Vintage PAPER TOYS

64 French models to make at home

SCRIPTUM
EDITIONS

THE PAPER TOY
CRAZE

Over the past few years, paper toys have made a major comeback. Free sites have popped up all over the internet. Children and adults alike are having fun making paper models of grinning robots, comic-strip heroes or small animals. Some people make collections of the finished models, while others decorate their offices with them or give them to friends and colleagues as presents. Simple, original and beguiling to look at, paper toys have secured the affections of a broad fan base and are currently hugely popular worldwide. But it would be a mistake to view this as merely the latest craft craze, as simply a matter of cutting printed shapes out of an A4 sheet and gluing them together. These designs are also a form of art that has its roots in origami, and that has been adopted by a wide variety of graphic designers whose imagination and talent has lent it new energy and impetus. One of the most celebrated artists currently working in this field is the young Japanese designer, Shin Tanaka, whose boundless creativity – standing at the interface of street culture, pop surrealism and low-brow – and growing reputation have earned him commissions from a number of major international brands. Another artist whose work is well known to paper toy aficionados is the French designer

Tougui. Both use their websites to showcase their latest creations.

'Paper toys' is a term that has recently been adopted internationally to describe a phenomenon with a long history. Models printed on paper, or card and designed to be cut out and folded, then slotted or glued together, have existed since the nineteenth century, when they were called 'paper cut-outs' or 'papercraft'. Popular with children of both sexes, these early designs were naturally very different from those of today. Nineteenth-century children had to be content with stock figures, based almost exclusively on soldiers and dolls that nowadays have a quaint if conventional charm.

The first printing house to mass-produce these paper cut-outs was the *Imagerie Epinal*, publishers of sentimental prints from Alsace, Lorraine and Germany. Having originally aimed its pious images chiefly at the faithful, in the early nineteenth century the business set out to appeal to a wider market. When Charles Nicolas Pellerin (1827–1887) inherited the *Imagerie Epinal*, he published numerous cut-out designs aimed principally at the British market, where paper dolls and their wardrobes became all the rage among small girls. From 1840, military figures were introduced for small boys to cut out. Still today, *Imagerie*

Epinal is famous for its numerous collections of cut-out designs, including its celebrated *Petit Architecte* series of 'major buildings' and 'minor buildings'. The huge variety of models available embraced a gondola and a windmill, a classroom and a harlequin, a fishermen's hüt and a Paris tram – all of them requiring just a few cuts and folds. Also popular were models in miniature of monuments both ancient modern, ranging from the *Palais du Trocadéro*, the Eiffel Tower and the Paris Opera to the house where Joan of Arc was born in the village of Domrémy. And a runaway success at this period was the paper toy theatre, with which children could make up their own scenarios by moving paper figures against a variety of often highly elaborate stage sets and backdrops.

By the early twentieth century, paper toys were an essential part of childhood. It wasn't long before advertisers began to hijacked them for their own purposes, producing models featuring the logos and slogans of many major brands. By appealing to children they aimed to secure the custom of their parents while also laying the ground for a future generation of customers. Up until the Second World War, major manufacturers such as Nestlé, Corona, Kellogs and Carnation commissioned toy makers to produce not only paper toys but also customized versions of board games such as snakes and ladders, jigsaws and silhouettes carrying their brand names. The phenomenon spread internationally, appearing not only in Europe, especially in France, Germany and Britain, but also in America, Canada and Japan. The 80 or so paper cut-outs that are featured here have been selected to reflect all the variety of twentieth-century French paper toys. Some are simple, others more complex: some were originally published in children's magazines, where they were were designed to appeal week by week to a young readership; most of were conceived as promotional gifts, to be given away free when a product was bought. But they all share the same detailed attention to their design. Just like the designers who excel today in the creation of paper toys, the illustrators who drew these paper cut-outs deployed all their talents in their work. Among them were children's book illustrators, who created popular series. In France one of the most famous is Benjamin Rabier, creator of *La Vache qui Rit*. Most of the artists remain in obscurity, however. The subjects they chose to depict reflect their times: in an age when toys were unashamedly gender-specific, small boys could gaze in wonder at jeeps and tanks, cars and lorries, trains, boats and planes, all based on real examples, while little girls could dress paper dolls, stage circus scenes or decorate Easter eggs.

In the 1950s plastic kits arrived, swiftly usurping the place of paper cut-outs and their publishers, who included Ingenia and Volumetrix in France, Schreiberg Verlag in Germany and Micromodels in Britain. But a few publishers continue to produce paper cut-outs to this day. In France, Domus and L'Instant Durable create magnificent card models of historic buildings and monuments, so perpetuating a fine creative tradition. And now this choice is vindicated by the new popularity that paper cut-outs are enjoying thanks to the internet. For all fans of this enduring art, it only remains to arm ourselves with scissors and glue before sampling this treasury of irresistible vintage paper toys.

CONTENTS

ELECTRIC TRUCK
(PLATE 1)

p. 11

(PLATE 2)

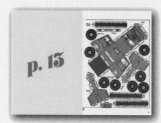

p. 13

NEWSPAPER VAN

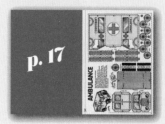

p. 15

AMBULANCE

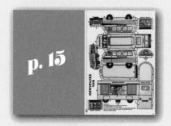

p. 17

HEAVY TANK
(PLATE 1)

p. 19

(PLATE 2)

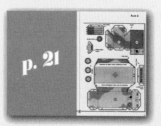

p. 21

HEAVY TANK (CONT.)
(PLATE 3)

p. 23

(PLATE 4)

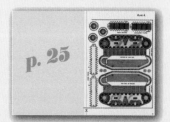

p. 25

BUILD YOUR OWN JEEP
(PLATE 1)

p. 27

(PLATE 2)

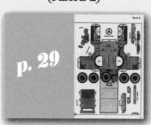

p. 29

SALOON CAR

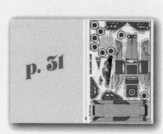

p. 31

CANDY TRUCK

p. 33

ALFA ROMEO GIULIA

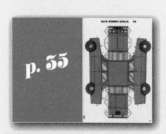

p. 35

**CLOWN AND
PERFORMING SEA LION**

p. 37

MERRY-GO-ROUND
(PLATE 1)

p. 39

(PLATE 2)

p. 41

MERRY-GO-ROUND (CONT.)
(PLATE 3)

p. 45

(PLATE 4)

p. 45

SUPER CIRCUS
(PLATE 1)

p. 47

(PLATE 2)

p. 49

ACROBAT

p. 51

TILLY THE DANCER AND
BANGO THE CLOWN

p. 55

DRESS UP DOLL

p. 55

DRESS UP LADY

p. 57

MARIE GOES FOR
A WALK

p. 59

DRESS UP
BOY AND GIRL

p. 61

REGIONAL COSTUMES

p. 65

SEDAN CHAIR

p. 65

PIVOTING CRANE

p. 67

STEAMROLLER

p. 69

WHEELBARROW

p. 71

RUBAN BLEU
RAILWAY STATION

p. 73

KITCHEN AND
RUSTIC COT

p. 75

COTTAGE AND GARDEN

p. 77

TABLE, STOOL AND BED

p. 79

MY COTTAGE

p. 81

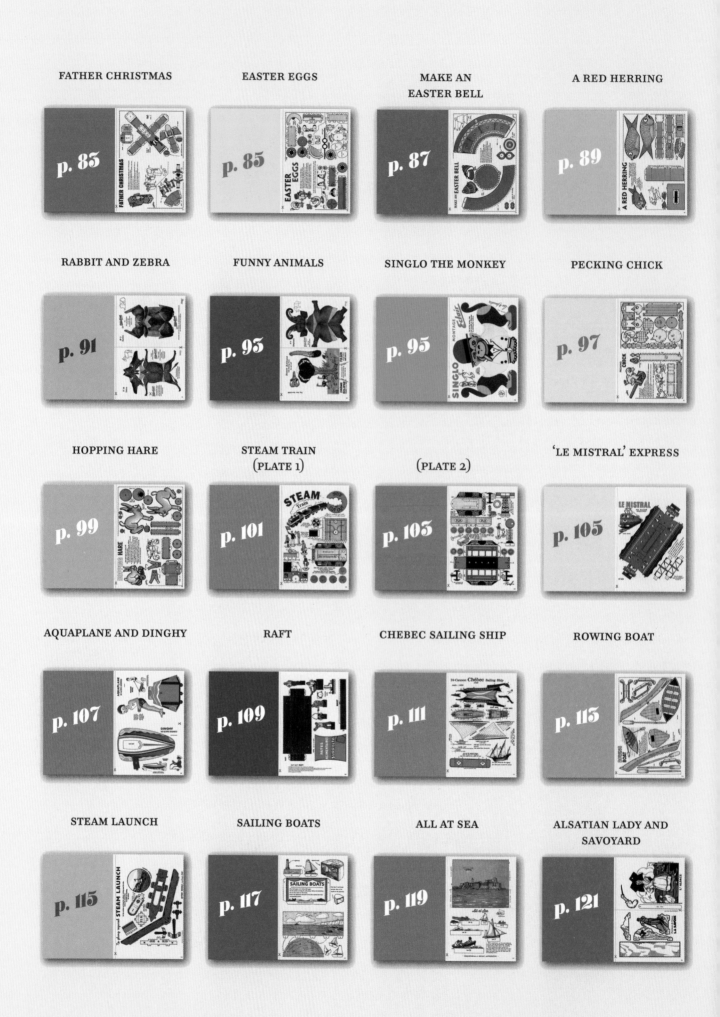

FATHER CHRISTMAS — p. 85

EASTER EGGS — p. 85

MAKE AN EASTER BELL — p. 87

A RED HERRING — p. 89

RABBIT AND ZEBRA — p. 91

FUNNY ANIMALS — p. 93

SINGLO THE MONKEY — p. 95

PECKING CHICK — p. 97

HOPPING HARE — p. 99

STEAM TRAIN (PLATE 1) — p. 101

(PLATE 2) — p. 103

'LE MISTRAL' EXPRESS — p. 105

AQUAPLANE AND DINGHY — p. 107

RAFT — p. 109

CHEBEC SAILING SHIP — p. 111

ROWING BOAT — p. 113

STEAM LAUNCH — p. 115

SAILING BOATS — p. 117

ALL AT SEA — p. 119

ALSATIAN LADY AND SAVOYARD — p. 121

MARKET TOWN

p. 123

WEDDING DAY

p. 125

COUNTRY CHURCH

p. 127

THE WOLF & THE LAMB

p. 129

TOM THUMB

p. 131

THE WOLF & THE CRANE

p. 133

SPACE EXPLORERS

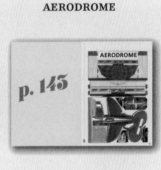
p. 135

TOY PLANE

p. 137

DOUGLAS DC-3 AIRCRAFT

p. 139

BUILD A LIGHT AIRCRAFT

p. 141

AERODROME

p. 143

WOOD-MILNE PAPER PLANE

p. 145

PIERRETTE PUPPET

p. 147

PUNCH PUPPET

p. 149

HARLEQUIN PUPPET

p. 151

MAKE YOUR OWN WOBBLY MAN

p. 153

PIGGY BANK (Plate 1)

p. 155

(Plate 2)

p. 157

PRACTICAL TIPS

This book contains some 80 vintage paper cut-out designs, including dolls, cars, animals, trains and planes. To make them, all you need is scissors, glue and – above all – patience. Novices are advised to start off with the simpler designs in order to get their hand in.

While scissors are all you need to cut round the designs, some of them contain areas that need cutting out, and for these you will also need a craft knife. Start by cutting roughly round the printed sections to make them easier to handle. Then cut along the outlines to create the final shapes. To make the folds follow the instructions on the design, scoring and bending along the dotted lines as indicated.

To glue the sections together, quick-setting liquid glue is easier to use than paste in a pot, which is awkward to spread. Take care not to let the glue spill over the edges of the tabs. Keep a small cloth handy so you can wipe your fingers and the paper if necessary, and avoid making marks on the designs.

Some of the cut-outs also require specific materials. The puppets on pages 147–52, for instance, need thread and brass paper fasteners, while the dinghy on page 107 requires a couple of corks.

A handy tip: scan the pages of your design into a computer, so if you make a mistake you can print them out on slightly stiff A4 paper and start again.

All the designs reproduced here are accompanied by detailed instructions. A little patience and application are therefore all you need to produce your own collection of authentic vintage paper toys.

ELECTRIC TRUCK

Le Hédan.

Glue both pages on to fairly stiff paper such as drawing paper. Cut out the sections along the black lines. Fold downwards on the dotted lines and upwards on the lines marked with crosses (++++).

Assemble each section separately by matching the letters in alphabetical order (A to A', B to B', etc.)

Assemble the sections together by matching the numbers in numerical order (1 to 1', 2 to 2', etc.).

Circles with dots in the middle indicate the position of axles (pins or matchsticks).

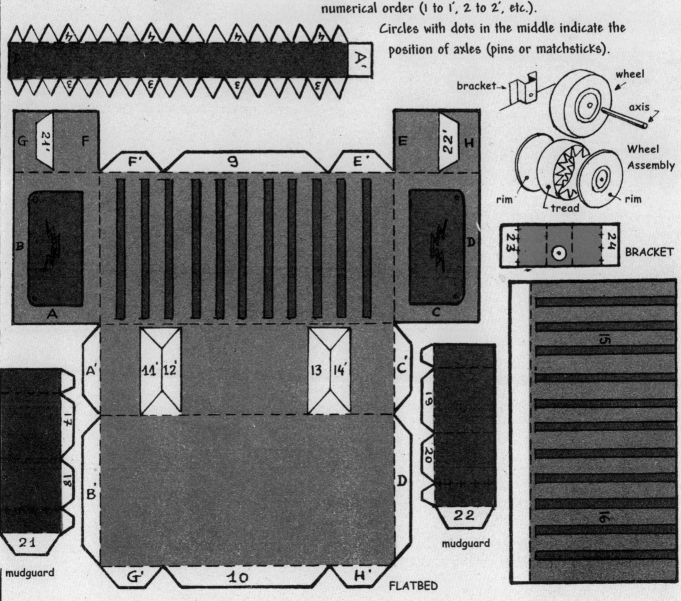

bracket → | wheel | axis

Wheel Assembly

rim | tread | rim

BRACKET | 23 | 24

FLATBED

mudguard

mudguard

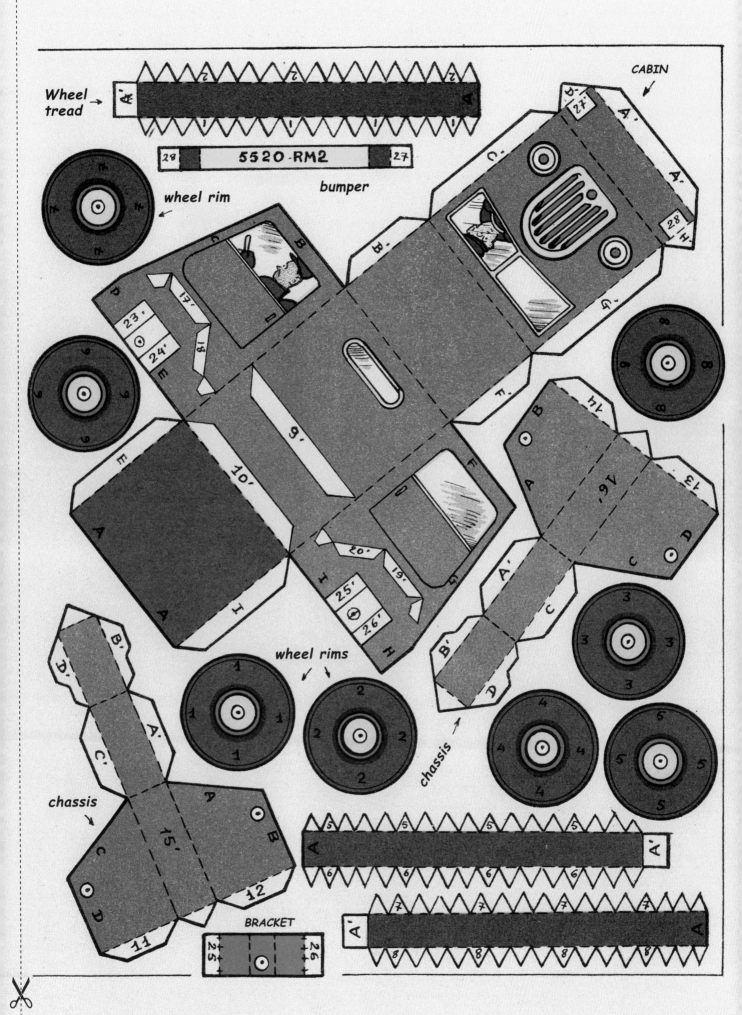

Wheel tread

wheel rim

bumper

5520-RM2

CABIN

wheel rims

chassis

chassis

BRACKET

13

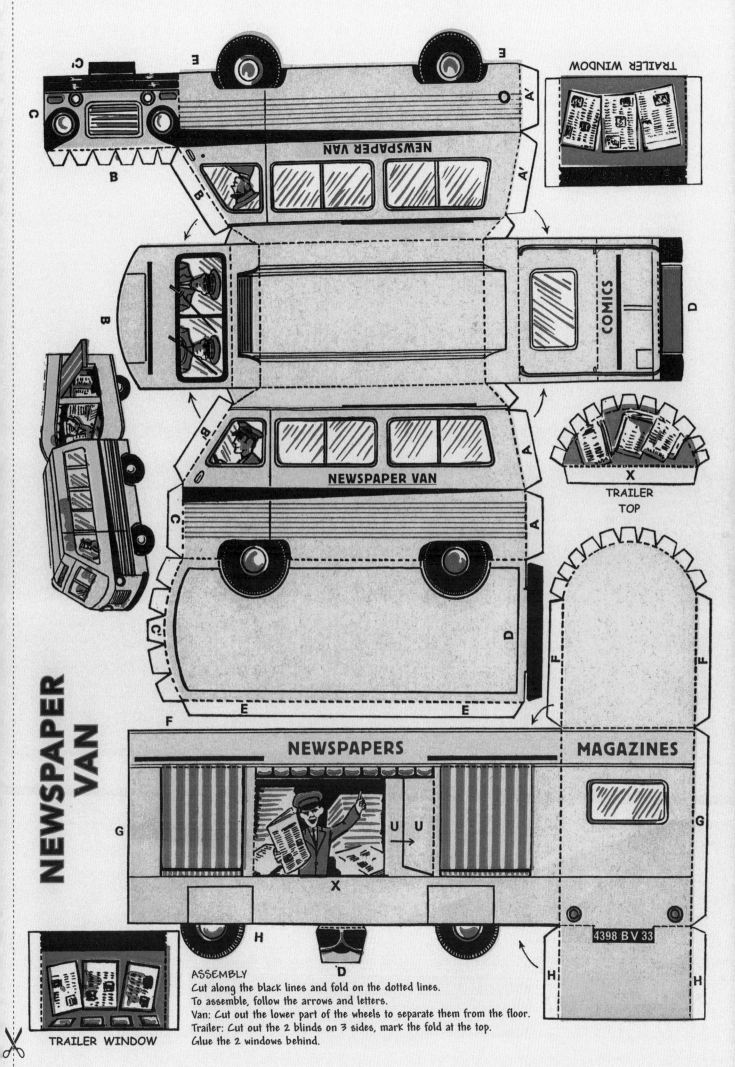

NEWSPAPER VAN

TRAILER WINDOW

NEWSPAPER VAN

COMICS

NEWSPAPER VAN

TRAILER TOP

X

NEWSPAPERS

MAGAZINES

TRAILER WINDOW

ASSEMBLY
Cut along the black lines and fold on the dotted lines.
To assemble, follow the arrows and letters.
Van: Cut out the lower part of the wheels to separate them from the floor.
Trailer: Cut out the 2 blinds on 3 sides, mark the fold at the top.
Glue the 2 windows behind.

4398 BV 33

15

AMBULANCE

Glue both pages on to fairly stiff paper such as drawing paper.
Cut the sections out along the black lines.
Fold downwards on the dotted lines and upwards on the lines marked with crosses (+++).
Assemble each section separately by matching the letters in alphabetical order (A to A', B to B', etc.).
Assemble the sections together by matching the numbers in numerical order (1 to 1', 2 to 2', etc.).
Circles with dots in the middle indicate the position of axles (matchsticks).

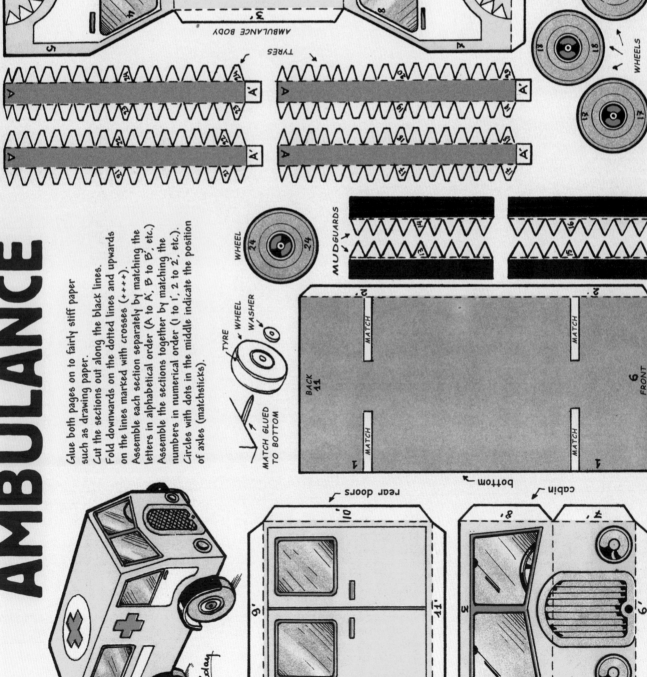

17

HEAVY TANK

PLATE 1.

Le Hédan

Glue both pages on to fairly stiff paper.
Cut all the sections out along the outlines.
Fold downwards on the dotted lines and upwards
on the lines marked with crosses (++++).
Cut out all parts marked with an X. Assemble each section separately by matching
the letters in alphabetical order (A to A', B to B', etc.) Assemble the sections
together by matching the numbers in numerical order (1 to 1', 2 to 2', etc.)

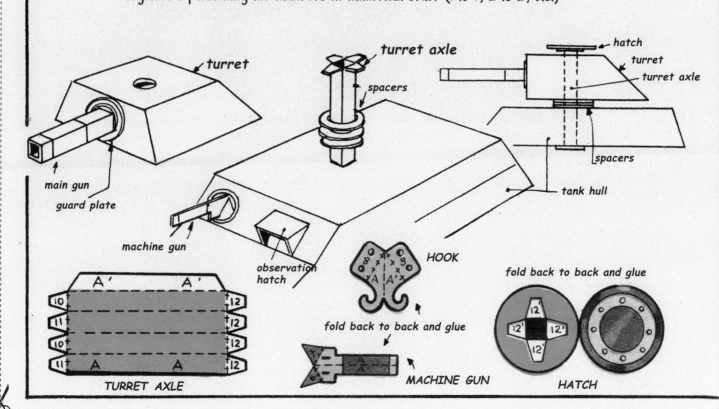

turret

turret axle

spacers

hatch
turret
turret axle

spacers

main gun
guard plate

machine gun

observation
hatch

tank hull

HOOK

fold back to back and glue

fold back to back and glue

A'   A'

10
11
10
11

12
12
12
12
12

A   A

TURRET AXLE

MACHINE GUN

12
12'   12'
12

HATCH

19

PLATE 2.

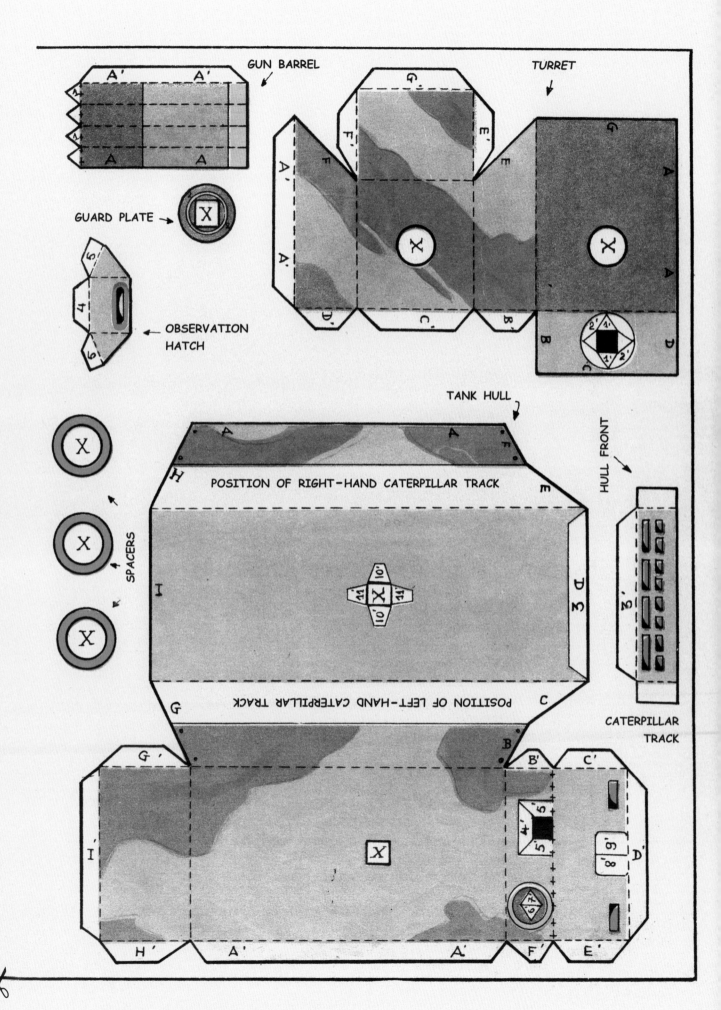

GUN BARREL

TURRET

GUARD PLATE

OBSERVATION HATCH

TANK HULL

SPACERS

POSITION OF RIGHT-HAND CATERPILLAR TRACK

HULL FRONT

POSITION OF LEFT-HAND CATERPILLAR TRACK

CATERPILLAR TRACK

HEAVY TANK (cont.)

PLATE 3.

Glue both pages on to fairly stiff paper.
Cut all the sections out along the outlines.
Fold downwards on the dotted lines and
upwards on the lines marked with crosses
(++++). Cut out all parts marked with an X.
Circles with dots in the middle indicate
the position of axles (rounded matchsticks).
Assemble each section separately by matching
the letters in alphabetical order (A to A', B to B', etc.).
Assemble the sections together by matching the numbers in
numerical order (1 to 1', 2 to 2', etc.).

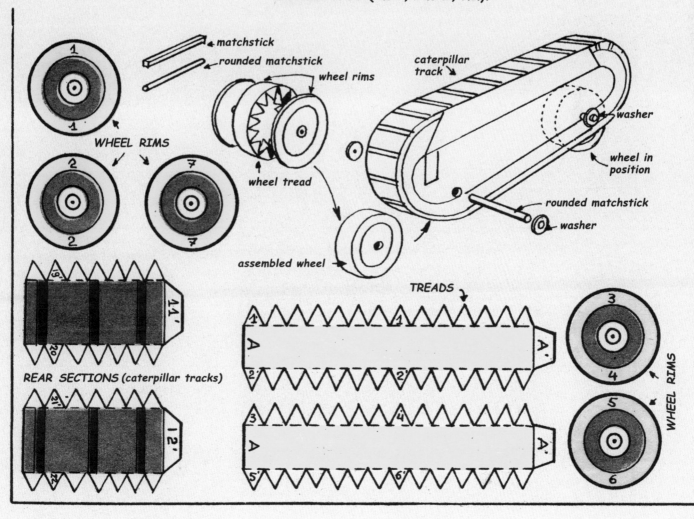

PLATE **4.**

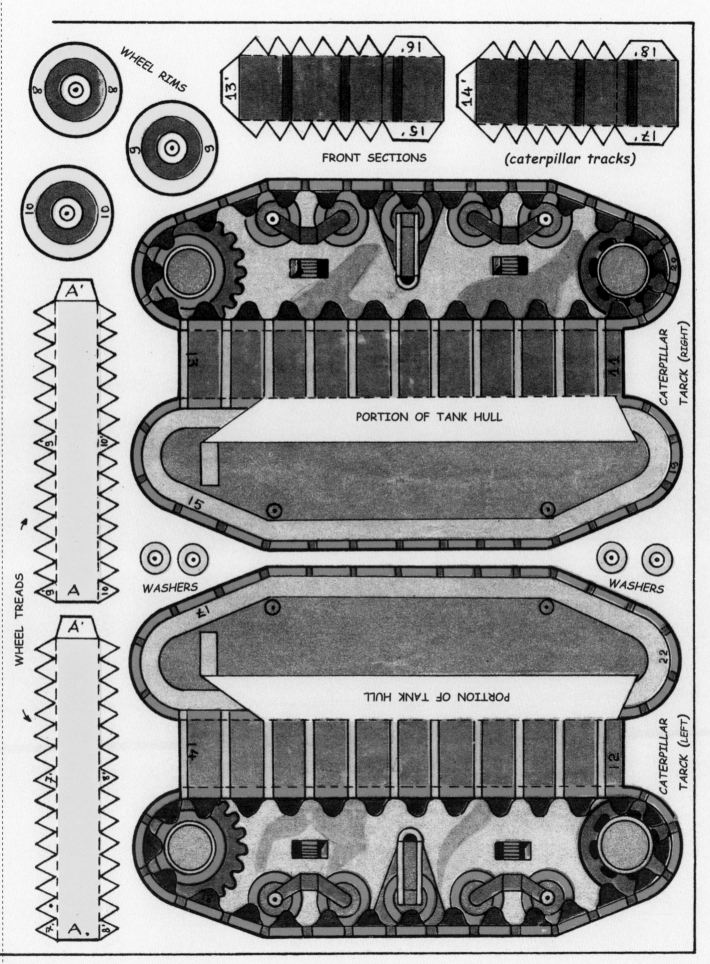

WHEEL RIMS

FRONT SECTIONS

(caterpillar tracks)

CATERPILLAR TARCK (RIGHT)

PORTION OF TANK HULL

CATERPILLAR TARCK (LEFT)

PORTION OF TANK HULL

WASHERS

WASHERS

WHEEL TREADS

BUILD YOUR OWN JEEP

PLATE 1.

1. GLUE BOTH PAGES ON TO THIN CARDBOARD OR DRAWING PAPER BEFORE CUTTING THEM OUT.
2. FOLD DOWNWARDS ON THE LINES MARKED WITH CROSSES (++++) AND UPWARDS ON THE DOTTED LINES. LIGHTLY SCORE USING A RULER AND CRAFT KNIFE TO OBTAIN SHARP CREASES.
3. ASSEMBLE THE SECTIONS BY MATCHING THE NUMBERS IN NUMERICAL ORDER (1 TO 1', 2 TO 2', ETC.).

cargo space   seats   windscreen   steering wheel   steering column   bonnet   bumper brackets   front bumper

FRONT SEATS

23   24   22   36' 33'   25   36

X indicates the floor vent at the driver's feet

BONNET

6'   29'   10   12'

53   8'   New York–Paris

5   CHASSIS TOP   15'   14   a cut out   a cut out   15

32   9   X   16

7'   13'

26'   11

PLATE 2.

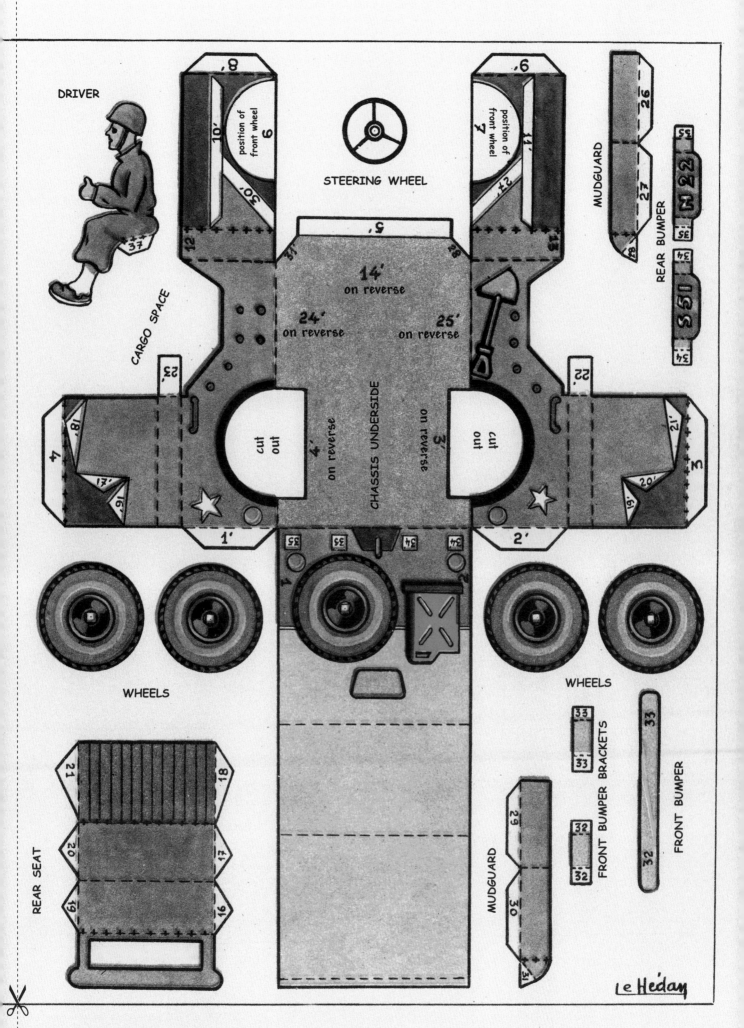

DRIVER

STEERING WHEEL

CARGO SPACE

MUDGUARD

REAR BUMPER

WHEELS

WHEELS

FRONT BUMPER BRACKETS

FRONT BUMPER

MUDGUARD

REAR SEAT

CHASSIS UNDERSIDE

Le Hédan

SALOON CAR

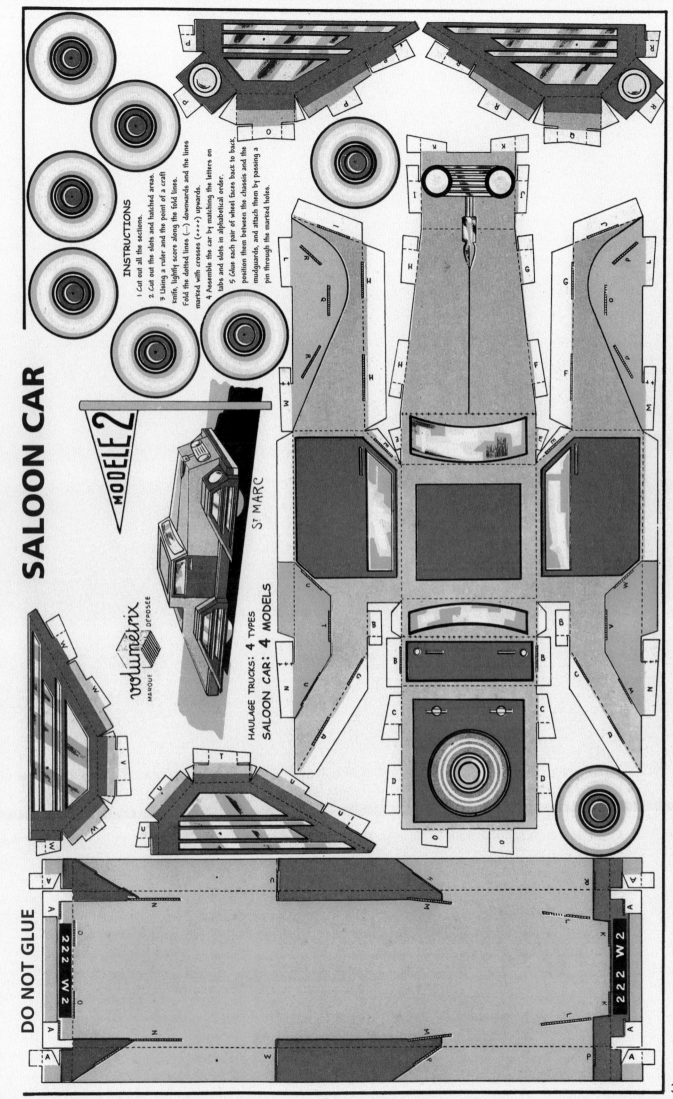

INSTRUCTIONS

1 Cut out all the sections.

2 Cut out the slots and hatched areas.

3 Using a ruler and the point of a craft knife, lightly score along the fold lines. Fold the dotted lines (----) downwards and the lines marked with crosses (++++) upwards.

4 Assemble the car by matching the letters on tabs and slots in alphabetical order.

5 Glue each pair of wheel faces back to back, position them between the chassis and the mudguards, and attach them by passing a pin through the marked holes.

MODELE 2

volumetrix MARQUE DEPOSEE

St MARC

HAULAGE TRUCKS: **4 TYPES**

SALOON CAR: **4 MODELS**

DO NOT GLUE

222 W2

222 W2

CANDY TRUCK

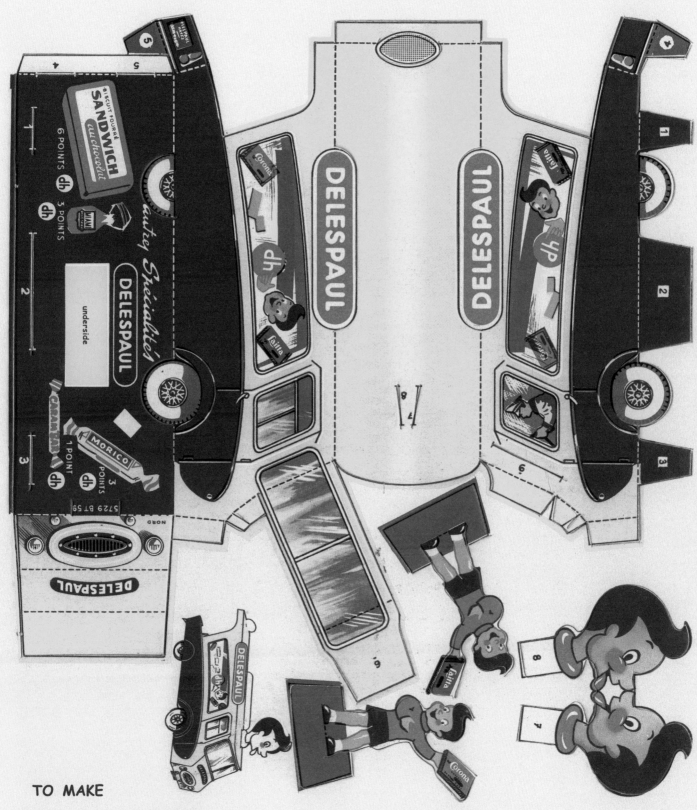

TO MAKE

1. Cut out the van and the figures.
2. Fold on the dotted lines.
3. Assemble by inserting the numbered tabs into the matching slots in order.

ALFA ROMEO GIULIA   VK

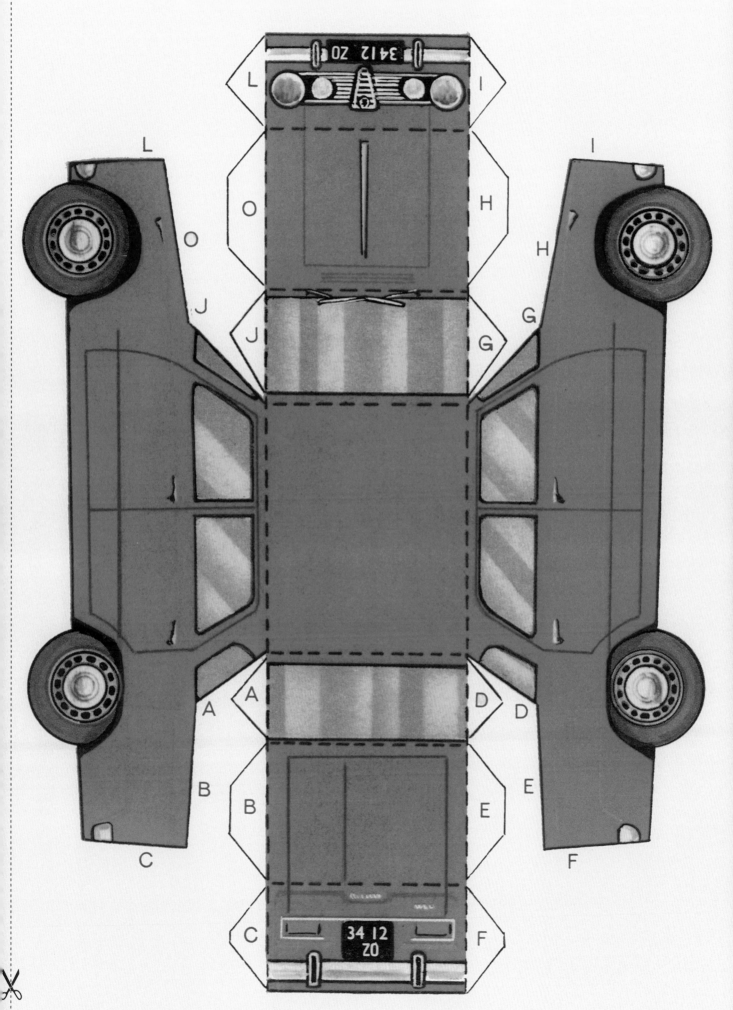

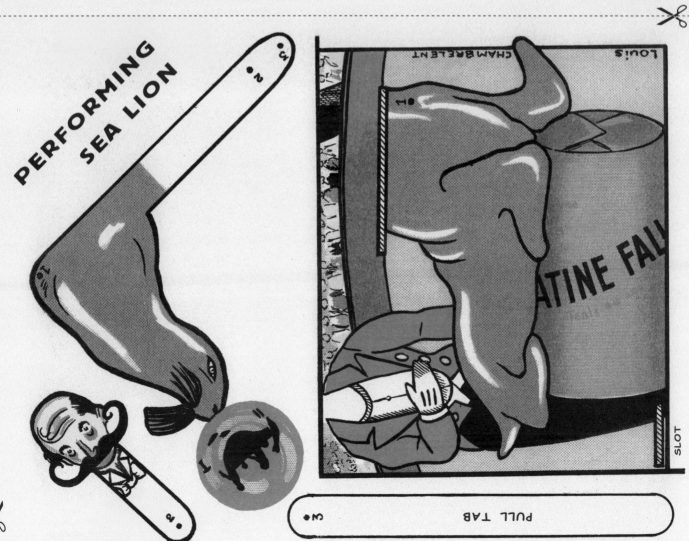

Merry-Go-Round

Take a strip of thin card Glue strip D to one end, and finally glue (as illustrated

measuring 2.5cm then glue C to A to the in sketch Y).

wide and 41 cm long. the hatched area D, hatched area B

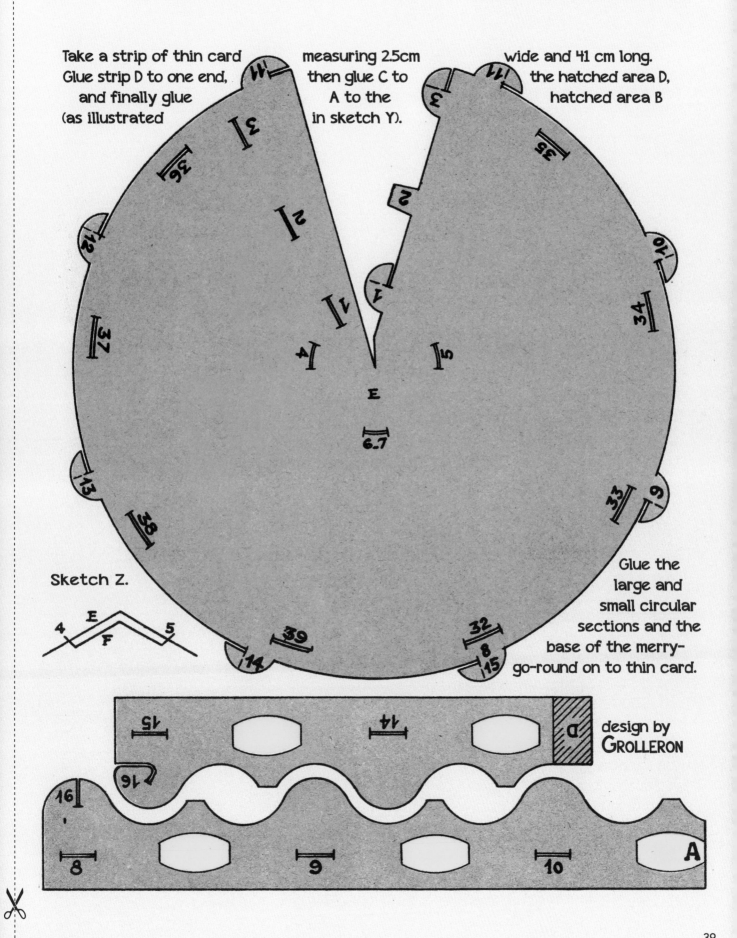

Sketch Z.

Glue the large and small circular sections and the base of the merry-go-round on to thin card.

design by GROLLERON

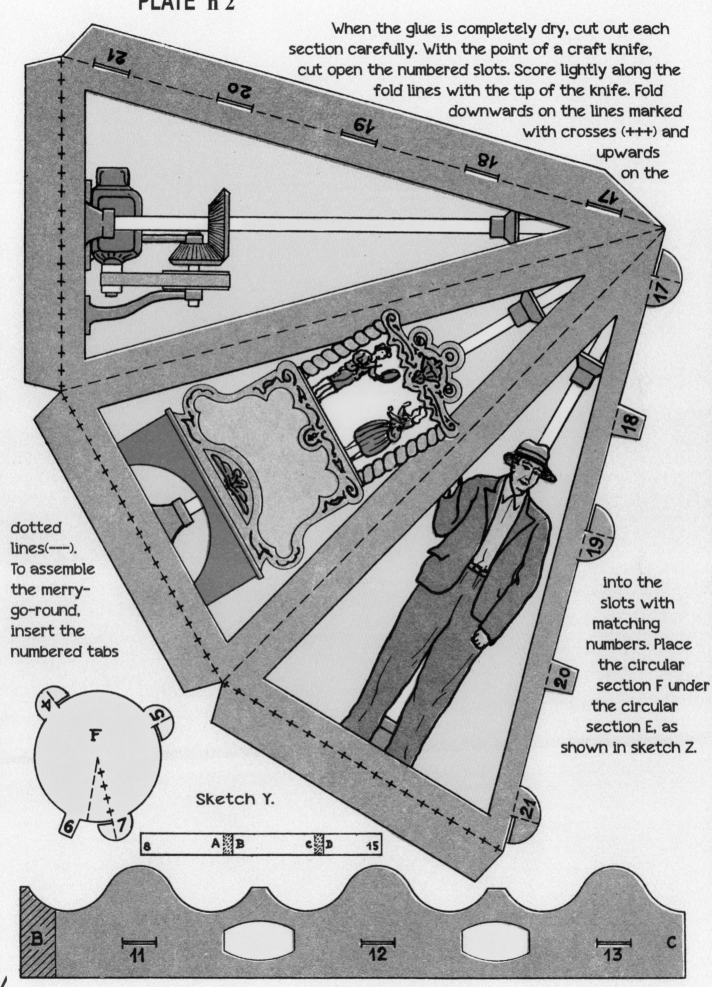

PLATE n°2

When the glue is completely dry, cut out each section carefully. With the point of a craft knife, cut open the numbered slots. Score lightly along the fold lines with the tip of the knife. Fold downwards on the lines marked with crosses (+++) and upwards on the

dotted lines(---). To assemble the merry-go-round, insert the numbered tabs

into the slots with matching numbers. Place the circular section F under the circular section E, as shown in sketch Z.

Sketch Y.

Merry-Go-Round (cont.)

Glue the circular section below on to thin card, then press between two books to dry. When the glue is completely dry, cut out the circle and remove the central section with its image of the finished model. Use the point of a craft knife to cut open the numbered slots, as well as slots 22 and 23 on plate 4.

Assemble the merry-go-round by inserting the tabs into their matching slots, working in numerical order.

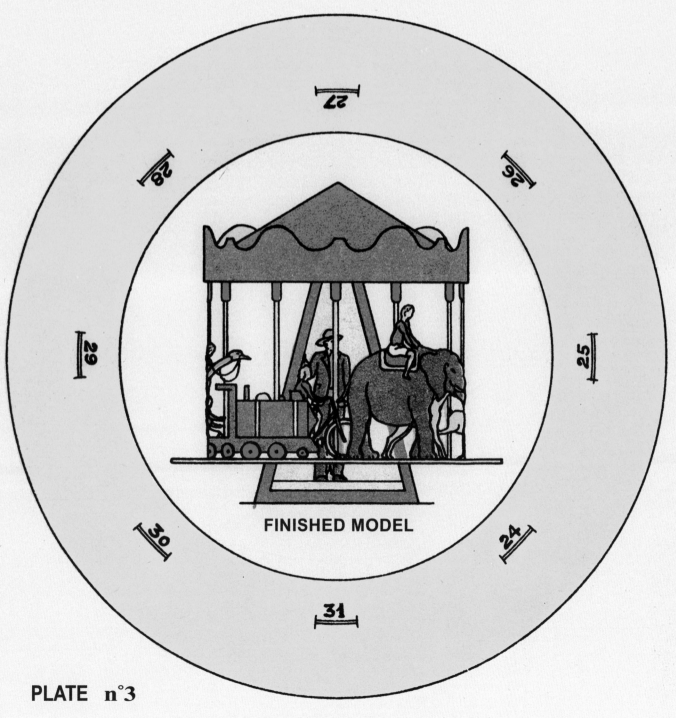

FINISHED MODEL

Glue these two strips on to a strip of card 40cm long,
cut them out, and glue G to the hatched area H.

PLATE n°4

45

47

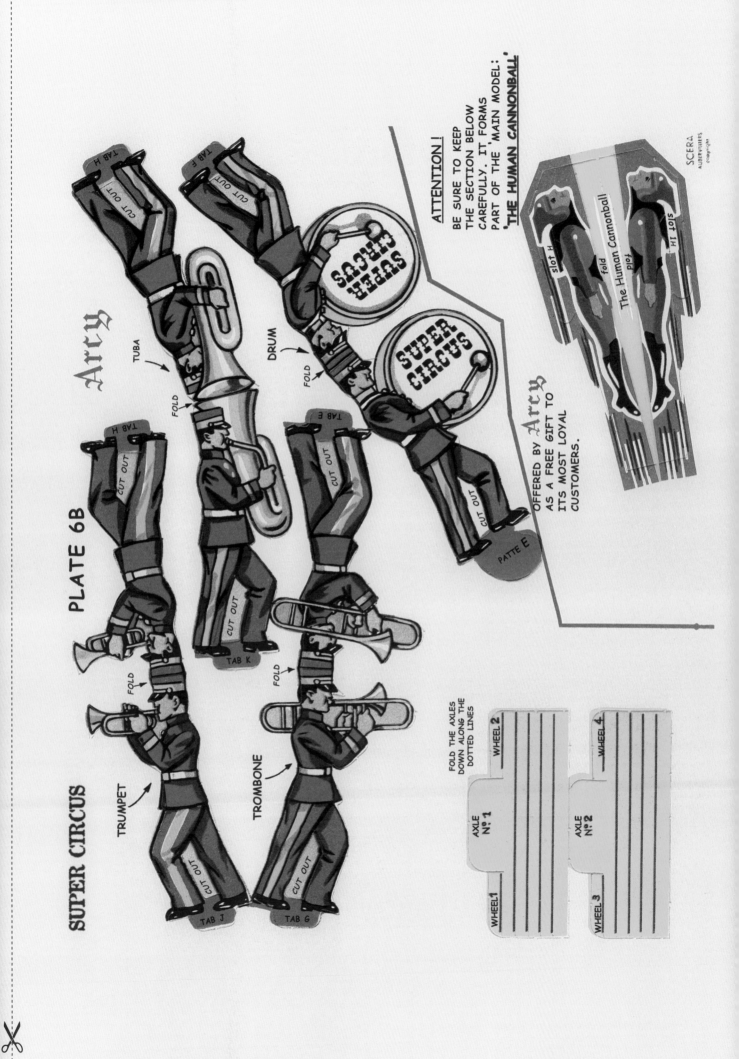

SUPER CIRCUS

PLATE 6B

Arty

SUPER CIRCUS

ATTENTION!

BE SURE TO KEEP
THE SECTION BELOW
CAREFULLY. IT FORMS
PART OF THE 'MAIN MODEL':
'THE HUMAN CANNONBALL'

OFFERED BY *Arty*
AS A FREE GIFT TO
ITS MOST LOYAL
CUSTOMERS.

The Human Cannonball

FOLD THE AXLES
DOWN ALONG THE
DOTTED LINES

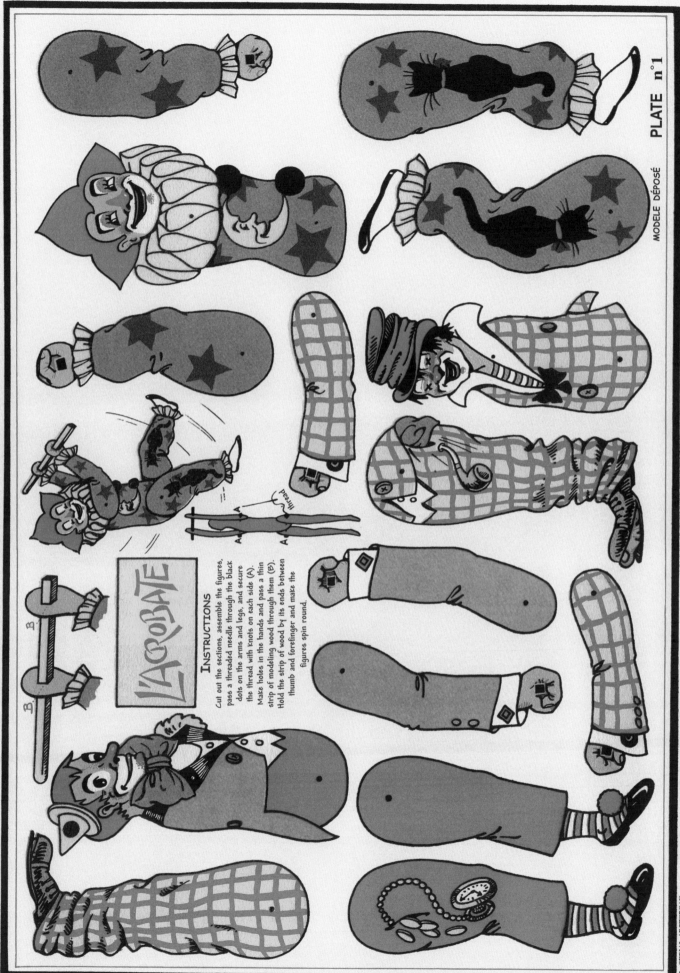

INSTRUCTIONS

Cut out the sections, assemble the figures, pass a threaded needle through the black dots on the arms and legs, and secure the thread with knots on each side (A). Make holes in the hands and pass a thin strip of modeling wood through them (B). Hold the strip of wood by its ends between thumb and forefinger and make the figures spin round.

L'ACROBATE

MODELE DÉPOSÉ

ÉDITIONS ARC-EN-CIEL, 57, Bd de Magenta, Paris.

IMP. CURIAL-ARCHEREAU.

TILLY

THE ACROBAT WITH STEEL TEETH

TO MAKE - Carefully cut out the sections and the holes within them. Make folds where marked. Gently widen the slots a little.

1. Insert the tab on the right leg into slot **A** on the body, then into slot **AA** on the left leg.

2. Insert the left arm into slot **B** on the body, up to the letter **B** on the arm.

3. Make the folds in the pulley, then insert tab **C** on the head into slots **C** and **CC** on the pulley. Pass a 60cm length of string through the pulley.

To make Tilly perform, hold the string as shown in the drawing, with one end higher then the other. She will slide from one end to the other.

PULLEY

BODY

LEFT LEG

RIGHT LEG

RIGHT ARM

LEFT ARM

③ BANGO THE DANCING CLOWN

TO MAKE - Carefully cut the sections and the holes within them. Make folds where marked. Gently widen the slots a little.

1. Insert tab **A** on the left leg into slot **A** on the body.

2. Insert tab **B** on the right leg into slot **B** on the body.

3. Attach the handle by inserting tab **C** into slot **C** from behind.

To make Bango perform, hold the end of the handle and move it up and down to make the clown dance (SEE ILLUSTRATION)

Poult **CIRCUS**

HOLD HERE

HANDLE

LEFT LEG

RIGHT LEG

BODY

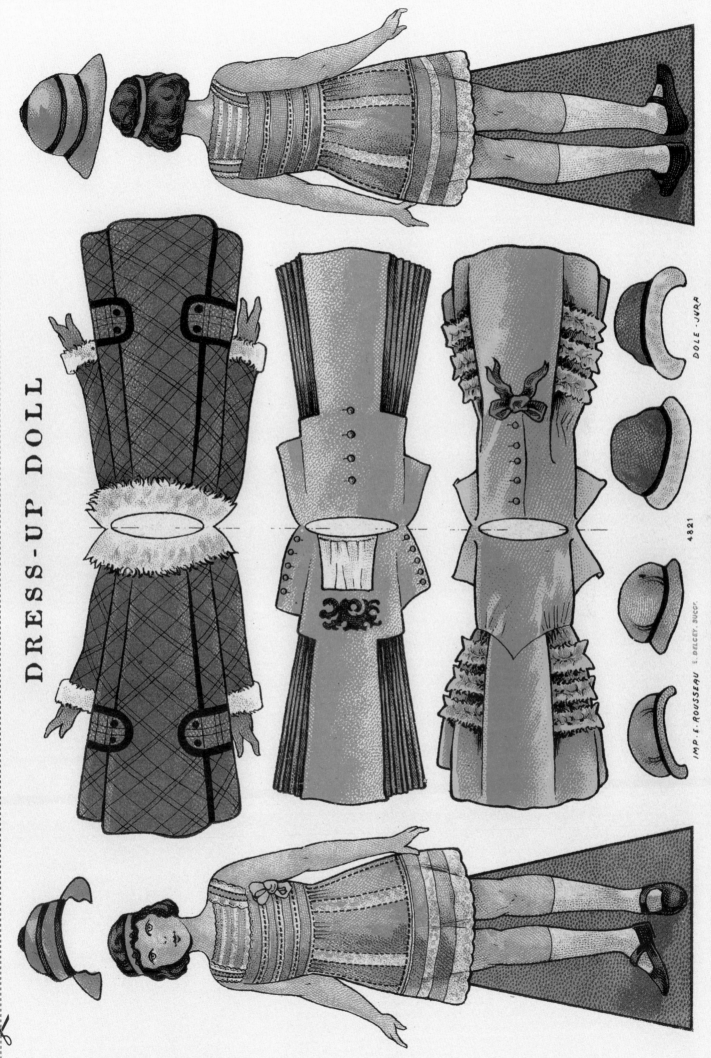

DRESS-UP DOLL

DOLE - JURA

IMP. E. ROUSSEAU E. DELCEY, SUCC'.

4821

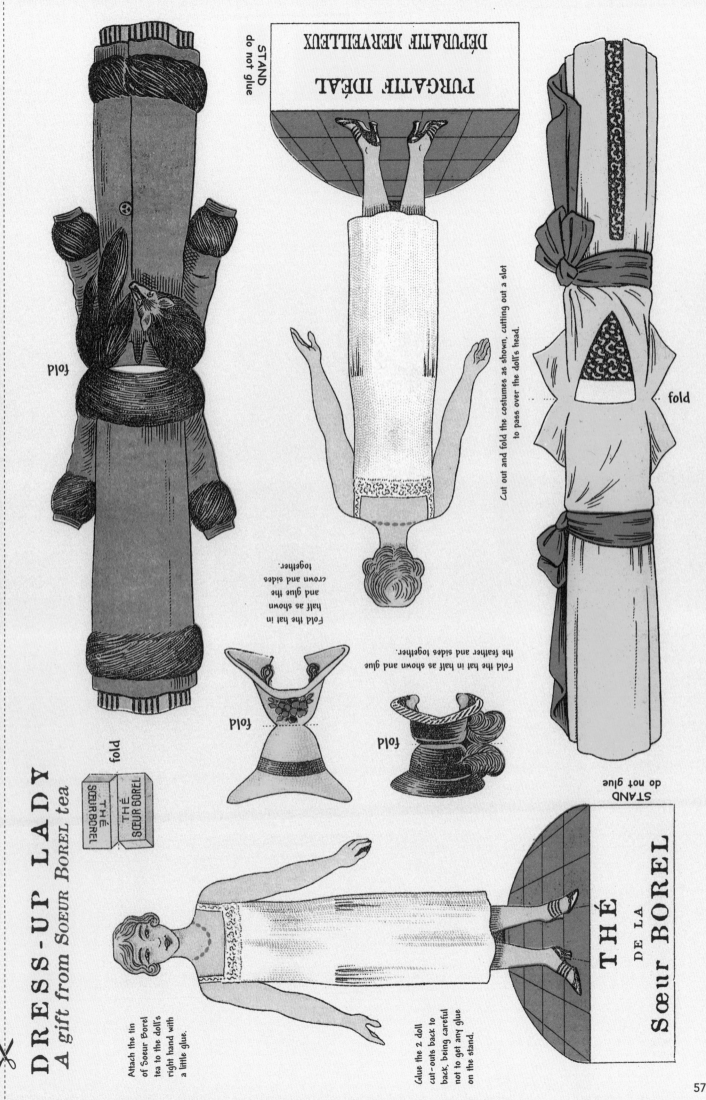

DRESS-UP LADY
A gift from Soeur Borel tea

Attach the tin of Soeur Borel tea to the doll's right hand with a little glue.

Glue the 2 doll cut-outs back to back, being careful not to get any glue on the stand.

fold

fold

fold

STAND
do not glue

PURGATIF IDEAL
DÉPURATIF MERVEILLEUX

Fold the hat in half as shown and glue the crown and sides together.

Fold the hat in half as shown and glue the feather and sides together.

Cut out and fold the costumes as shown, cutting out a slot to pass over the doll's head.

fold

fold

fold

THÉ SŒUR BOREL

THÉ SŒUR BOREL

STAND
do not glue

THÉ
DE LA
SŒUR BOREL

57

MARIE GOES FOR A WALK   EL PASEO DE LOLITA

para doblar
para agujerear
patas para introducir en los agujeros

----- fold
⎯ cut
▮ tabs to be placed in slots

MODEL

59

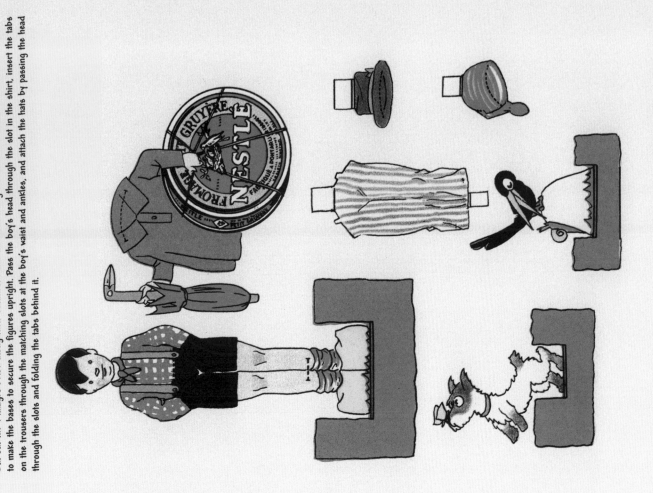

Cut out the 5 images along their outlines. Make incisions along the dotted lines. Fold along the double lines to make the bases to secure the figures upright. Pass the girl's head through the slot in the shawl. To attach the shawl, slot the tabs through the matching slots at the girl's waist and feet.

DRESS-UP BOY & GIRL

Cut out the 7 images below along their outlines. Make incisions along the dotted lines. Fold on the double lines to make the bases to secure the figures upright. Pass the boy's head through the slot in the shirt, insert the tabs on the trousers through the matching slots at the boy's waist and ankles, and attach the hats by passing the head through the slots and folding the tabs behind it.

REGIONAL COSTUMES

1 ALSACE 3 ANGOUMOIS
2 PROVENCE·NICE 4 BOURGOGNE

JEAN. MAUGUIÈRE – IMP. PARIS.

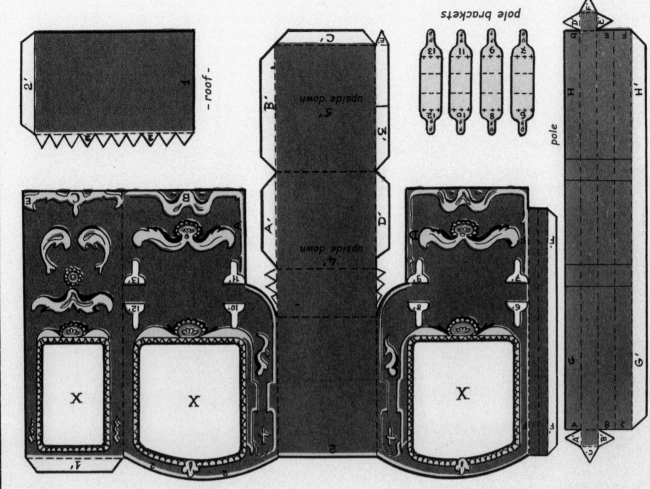

SEDAN CHAIR

Glue both pages on to fairly stiff paper such as drawing paper. Carefully cut the sections out along the outlines. Fold downwards on the dotted lines and upwards on the lines marked with crosses (++++).

Assemble each section separately by matching the letters in alphabetical order (A to A', B to B', etc.). Assemble the sections together by matching the numbers in numerical order (1 to 1', 2 to 2', etc.).

Cut out areas marked with an X.

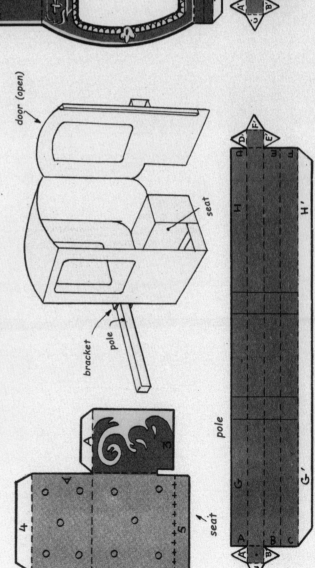

- roof -

pole brackets

pole

upside down

upside down

door (open)

seat

bracket

pole

seat

pole

PIVOTING CRANE

Glue both pages on to fairly stiff paper such as drawing paper.

Cut the sections out along the outlines.

Fold downwards on the dotted lines and upwards on the lines marked with crosses (+++).

Assemble the sections separately by matching the letters in alphabetical order (A to A1, B to B1, etc.)

Assemble the sections together by matching the numbers in numerical order (1 to 11, 2 to 21, etc.).

Cut out areas marked with an X.

Circles with dots ⊙ in the middle indicate the position of axles (pins or matchsticks).

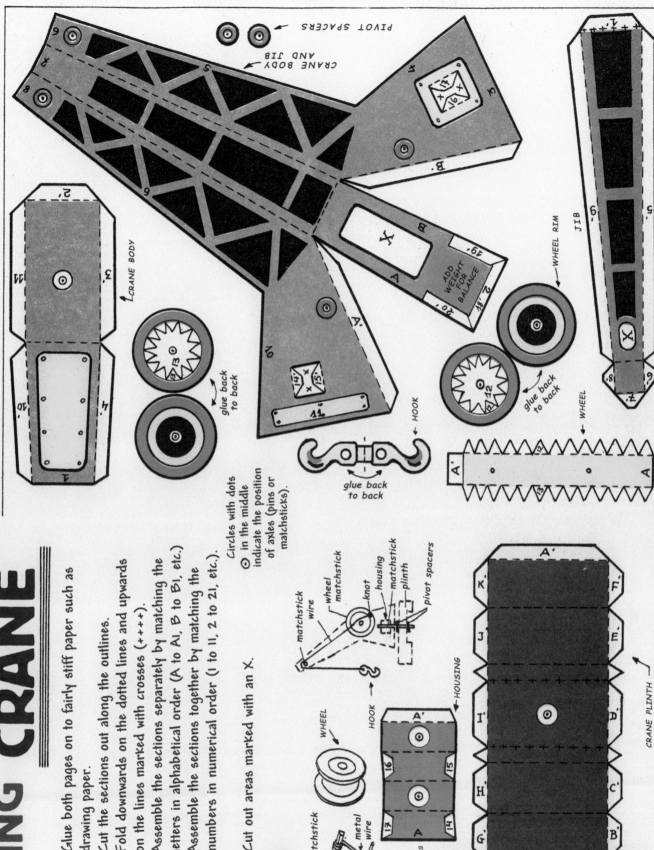

PIVOT SPACERS

CRANE BODY AND JIB

ADD WEIGHT FOR BALANCE

CRANE BODY

glue back to back

HOOK

glue back to back

WHEEL RIM

JIB

WHEEL

glue back to back

WHEEL

A

HOOK

glue back to back

matchstick
wire
wheel
matchstick
knot
housing
matchstick
plinth
pivot spacers

HOUSING

WHEEL

HOOK

COUNTERWEIGHTS

matchstick

metal wire

HAND WINCH

CRANE PLINTH

STEAMROLLER

Glue both pages on to fairly stiff paper such as drawing paper.

Cut the sections out along the outlines.

Fold downwards on the dotted lines and upwards on the lines marked with crosses (+++).

Assemble each section separately by matching the letters in alphabetical order (A to A', B to B', etc.).

Assemble the sections together by matching the numbers in numerical order (1 to 1', 2 to 2', etc.).

Circles with dots in the middle indicate the position ⊙ of axles (matchsticks).

matchsticks

axle forks

matchsticks

WHEEL

washer

cork

roller

CABIN

glue back to back

ROLLER

AXLE FORKS

Le Hédan

FUNNEL

body →

axle forks

WHEEL

glue back to back

WHEEL

glue back to back

cork

cork

CABIN

WASHERS

roller

A

B

C

A'

A

A

A'

A'

CABIN

ROLLER

AXLE FORKS

MAKE YOUR OWN WHEELBARROW

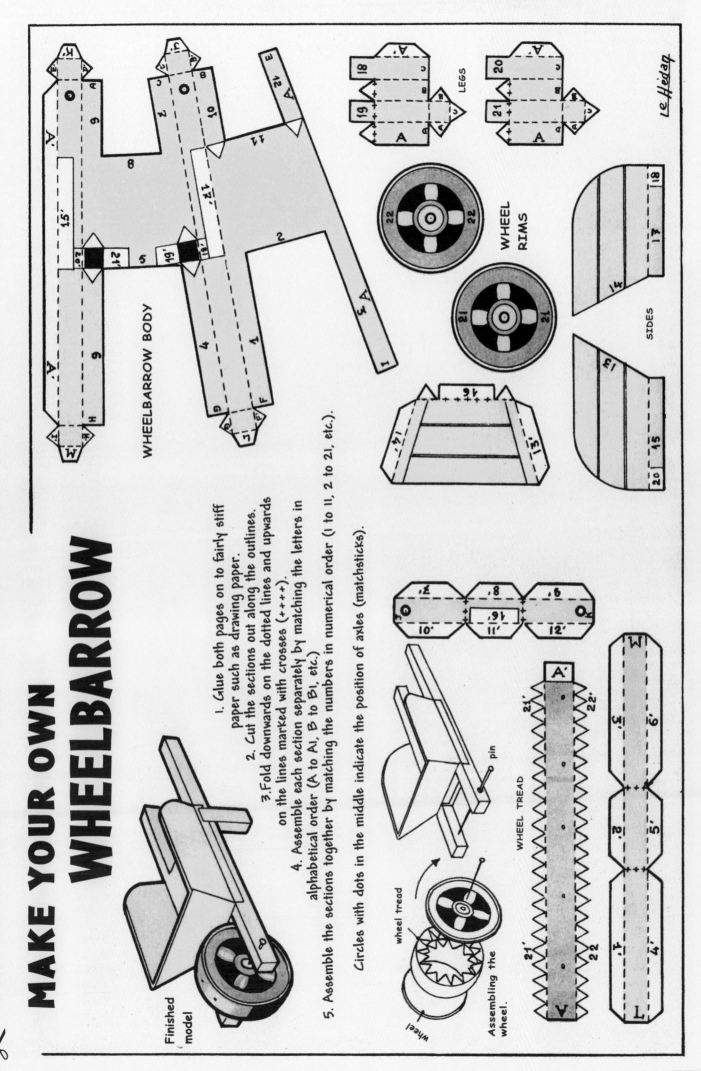

Finished model

WHEELBARROW BODY

LEGS

WHEEL RIMS

SIDES

WHEEL TREAD

Assembling the wheel.

wheel tread

pin

wheel

1. Glue both pages on to fairly stiff paper such as drawing paper.
2. Cut the sections out along the outlines.
3. Fold downwards on the dotted lines and upwards on the lines marked with crosses (+++).
4. Assemble each section separately by matching the letters in alphabetical order (A to A1, B to B1, etc.)
5. Assemble the sections together by matching the numbers in numerical order (1 to 11, 2 to 21, etc.).

Circles with dots in the middle indicate the position of axles (matchsticks).

Le Hedap

71

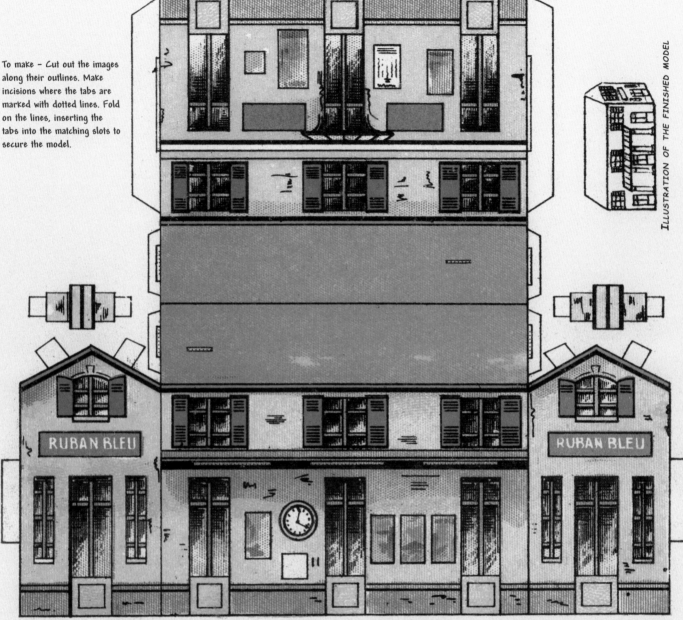

To make – Cut out the images along their outlines. Make incisions where the tabs are marked with dotted lines. Fold on the lines, inserting the tabs into the matching slots to secure the model.

RUBAN BLEU

RUBAN BLEU

MARGARINE

RUBAN BLEU

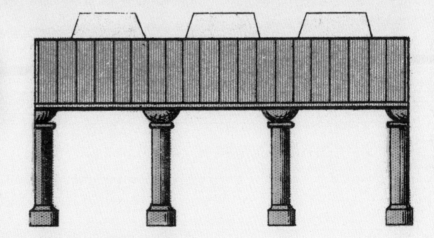

RAILWAY STATION

TOYS FROM THE
LOTERIE NATIONALE

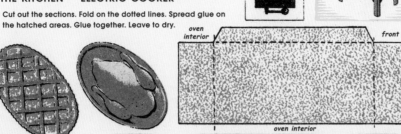

THE KITCHEN – ELECTRIC COOKER

Cut out the sections. Fold on the dotted lines. Spread glue on the hatched areas. Glue together. Leave to dry.

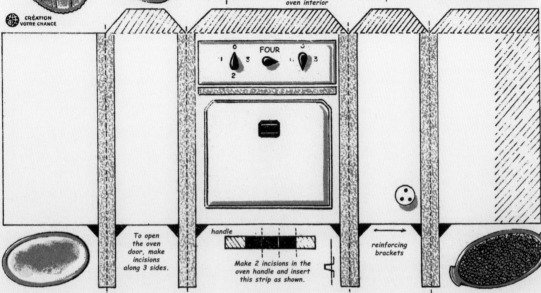

CRÉATION VOTRE CHANCE

oven interior

front

oven interior

FOUR

0 1 2 3

To open the oven door, make incisions along 3 sides.

handle

Make 2 incisions in the oven handle and insert this strip as shown.

reinforcing brackets

TOYS FROM THE
LOTERIE NATIONALE

THE BEDROOM – RUSTIC COT

Cut out the sections. Fold on the dotted lines. Glue tabs A to the head of the cot, and tabs B to the inside of the foot. Make the rockers (C). Insert the struts (D and E).

Use a small piece of cloth to make the cover.

FOOT

HEAD

A A A

D D D D D D

E E E E E E

C C

UNDERSIDE

B B

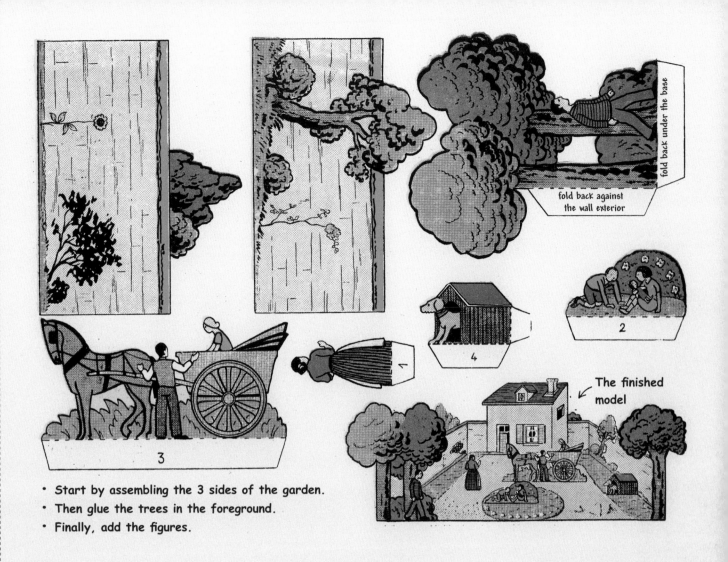

fold back under the base

fold back against the wall exterior

2

4

1

3

The finished model

- Start by assembling the 3 sides of the garden.
- Then glue the trees in the foreground.
- Finally, add the figures.

COTTAGE & GARDEN

- Glue both pages on to fairly stiff paper.
- Cut out the sections.
- Fold on the dotted lines.

fold back against the wall exterior

fold back under the base

1

3

2

4

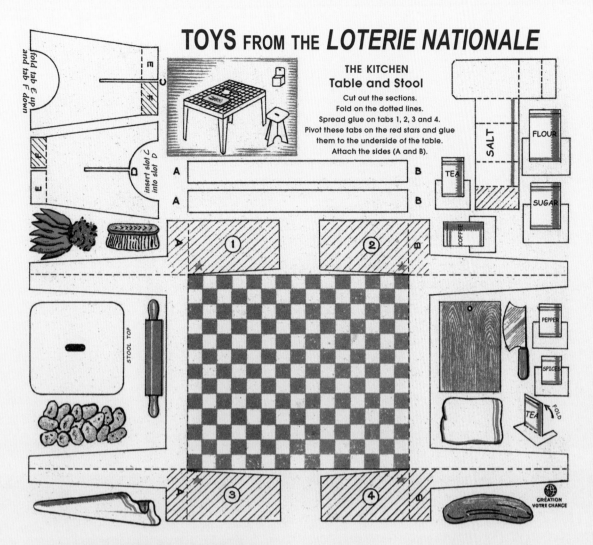

TOYS FROM THE *LOTERIE NATIONALE*

THE KITCHEN
Table and Stool

Cut out the sections.
Fold on the dotted lines.
Spread glue on tabs 1, 2, 3 and 4.
Pivot these tabs on the red stars and glue
them to the underside of the table.
Attach the sides (A and B).

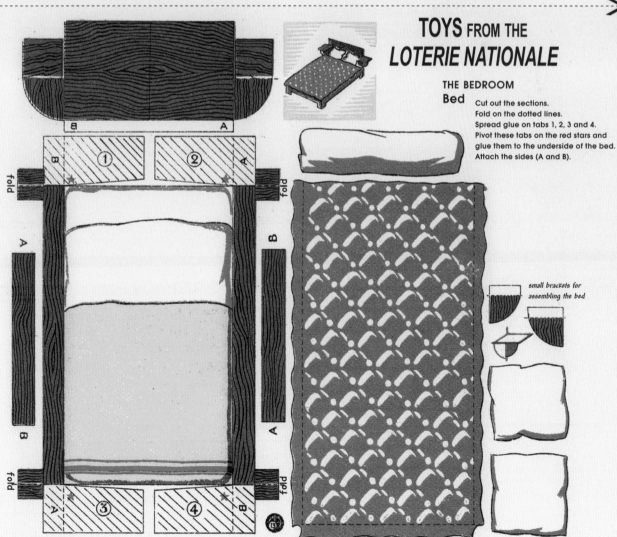

TOYS FROM THE
LOTERIE NATIONALE

THE BEDROOM
Bed

Cut out the sections.
Fold on the dotted lines.
Spread glue on tabs 1, 2, 3 and 4.
Pivot these tabs on the red stars and
glue them to the underside of the bed.
Attach the sides (A and B).

small brackets for assembling the bed

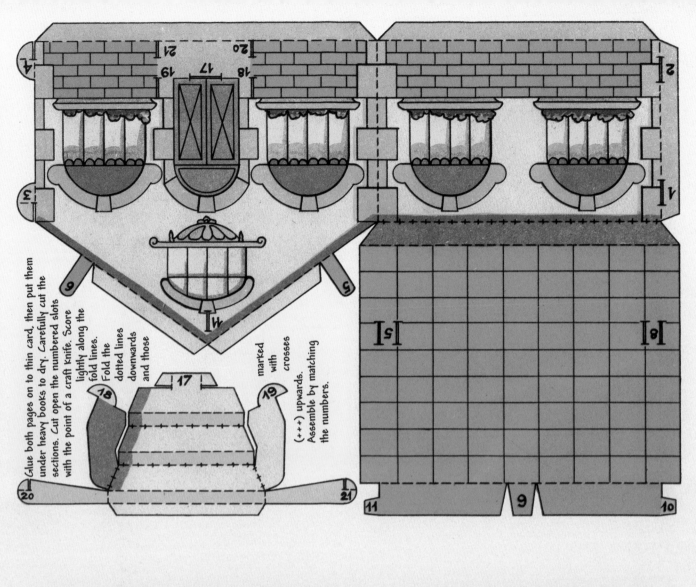

Glue both pages on to thin card, then put them under heavy books to dry. Carefully cut the sections. Cut open the numbered slots with the point of a craft knife. Score lightly along the fold lines. Fold the dotted lines downwards and those marked with crosses (+++) upwards. Assemble by matching the numbers.

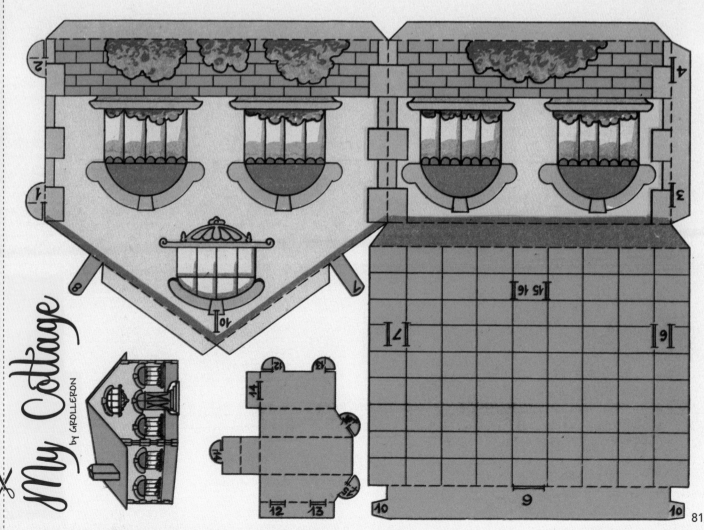

My Cottage by GROLLERON

FATHER CHRISTMAS

Glue both pages on to fairly stiff paper such as drawing paper.
Cut out the sections out along the outlines.
Fold downwards on the dotted lines and upwards on the lines marked with crosses (+++).
Assemble each section separately by matching the letters in alphabetical order (A to A', B to B', etc.)
Assemble the sections together by matching the numbers in numerical order (1 to 1', 2 to 2', etc.).

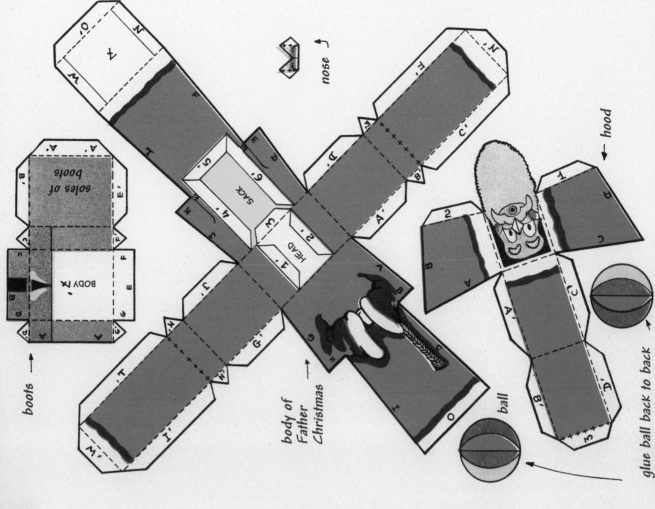

boots →

soles of boots

BODY K'

body of Father Christmas →

SACK

HEAD

nose →

hood →

ball

glue ball back to back →

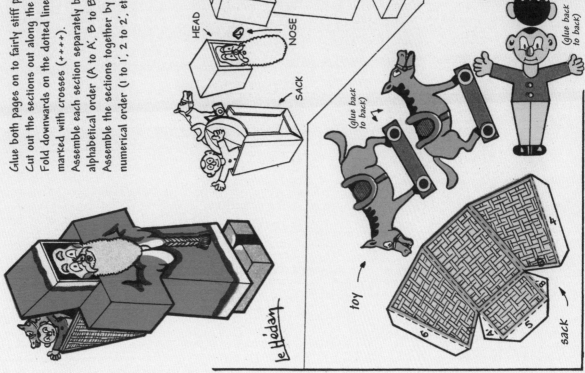

le Hédan

HEAD

BODY

SACK

NOSE

BOOTS

(glue back to back)

(glue back to back)

toy →

sack →

toy →

(glue back to back)

83

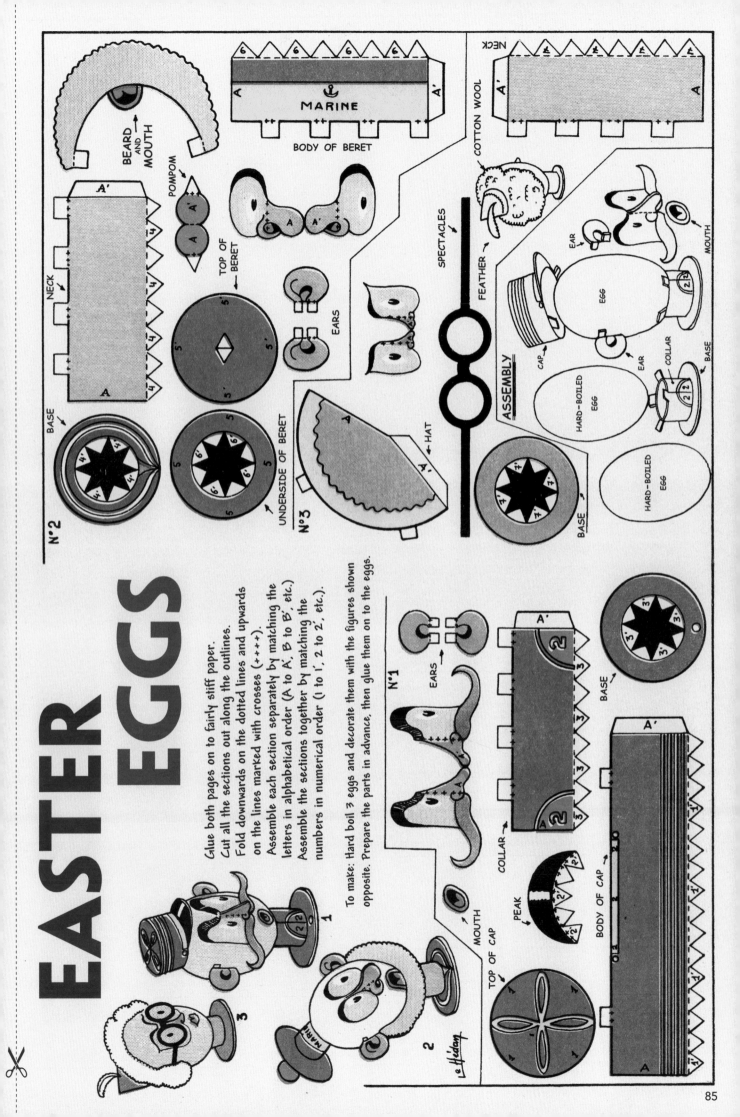

EASTER EGGS

Glue both pages on to fairly stiff paper.
Cut all the sections out along the outlines.
Fold downwards on the dotted lines and upwards
on the lines marked with crosses (+++).
Assemble each section separately by matching the
letters in alphabetical order (A to A', B to B', etc.)
Assemble the sections together by matching the
numbers in numerical order (1 to 1', 2 to 2', etc.).

To make: Hard boil 3 eggs and decorate them with the figures shown
opposite. Prepare the parts in advance, then glue them on to the eggs.

BEARD AND MOUTH

BODY OF BERET

MARINE

COTTON WOOL

NECK

POMPOM

TOP OF BERET

EARS

NECK

BASE

UNDERSIDE OF BERET

N°3

← HAT

SPECTACLES

FEATHER

ASSEMBLY

CAP

EAR

EGG

EAR

MOUTH

HARD-BOILED EGG

COLLAR

BASE

HARD-BOILED EGG

BASE

N°2

EARS →

N°1

COLLAR

MOUTH

PEAK

TOP OF CAP

BODY OF CAP

BASE

A'

A'

A'

Le Hiday

MAKE AN EASTER BELL

ring
bell
eyelet
box
box base

TOP VIEW OF BELL

BELL

RING

cut out
cut out

Le Hedan

Glue both pages on to fairly stiff
paper such as drawing paper.
Cut all the sections out along the outlines.
Fold downwards on the dotted lines and
upwards on the lines marked with crosses (++++).
Assemble the sections by matching the numbers
in numerical order (1 to 1', 2 to 2', etc.).
Fill the box with sweets to make an attractive
Easter gift for friends and family.

BOX BASE

BOX

eyelets for threading
ribbons

A RED HERRING

Glue both pages on to fairly stiff paper such as drawing paper.
Carefully cut all the sections out along the outlines.
Fold downwards on the dotted lines and upwards on the lines marked with crosses (+++). Make the spine by gluing X to X' and Y to Y'.

Then assemble the sections together by matching the numbers in numerical order (1 to 1', 2 to 2', etc.).

Fill this box with sweets to make an attractive gift for friends and family.

BOX →

BASE ↘

fish
box
base

FINS

glue back to back

spine

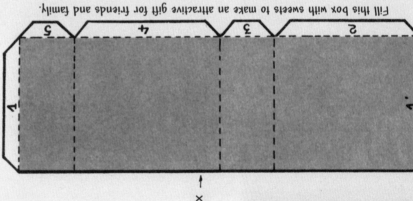
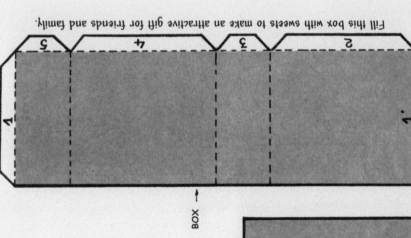
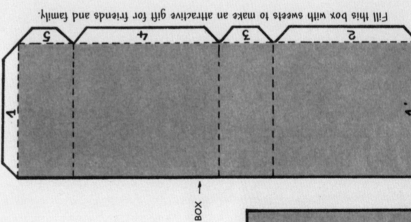
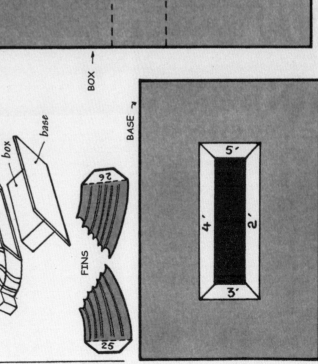

Lettricday

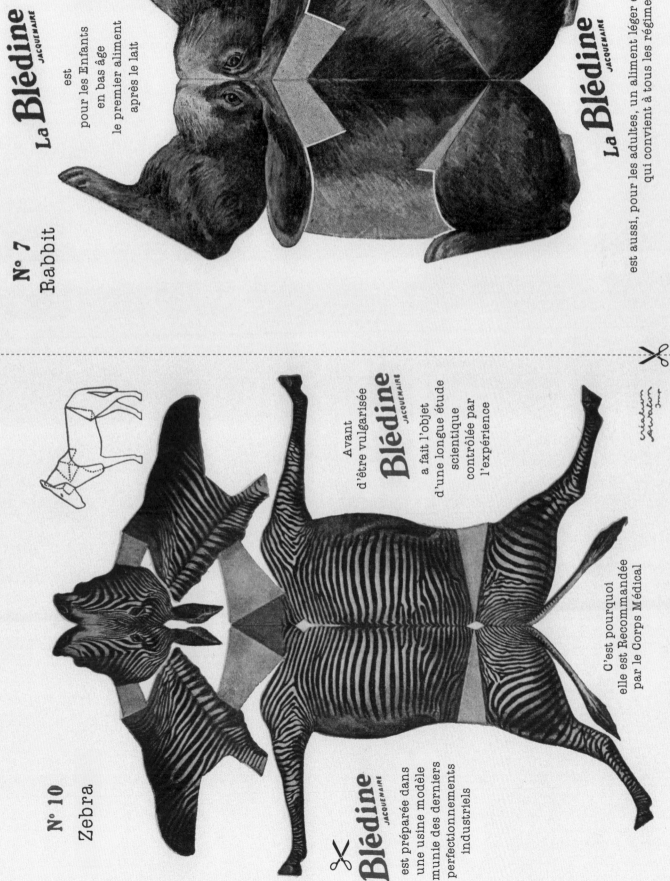

N° 7
Rabbit

La **Blédine** JACQUEMAIRE

est
pour les Enfants
en bas âge
le premier aliment
après le lait

La **Blédine** JACQUEMAIRE

est aussi, pour les adultes, un aliment léger et reconstituant
qui convient à tous les régimes

N° 10
Zebra

Avant
d'être vulgarisée
Blédine JACQUEMAIRE
a fait l'objet
d'une longue étude
scientifique
contrôlée par
l'expérience

C'est pourquoi
elle est Recommandée
par le Corps Médical

Blédine JACQUEMAIRE

est préparée dans
une usine modèle
munie des derniers
perfectionnements
industriels

91

N°3
Elephant

Blédine
JACQUEMAIRE

fait les
Bébés robustes

FUNNY ANIMALS
with Moving Parts
(to cut out)

Reg. Com. Seine 59.808

FULGOR
POUR TOUS
MÉTAUX

cut here

Fold this section
down and those to
either side up.

cut here

**CRÈME
ÉCLIPSE**
CIRAGE A LA CIRE

MONTAGE *Éclair

Cut out the monkey, fold
and assemble as illustrated
by matching the numbers.

SINGLO

ÉDITÉ PAR
Éd. H. Jeudia

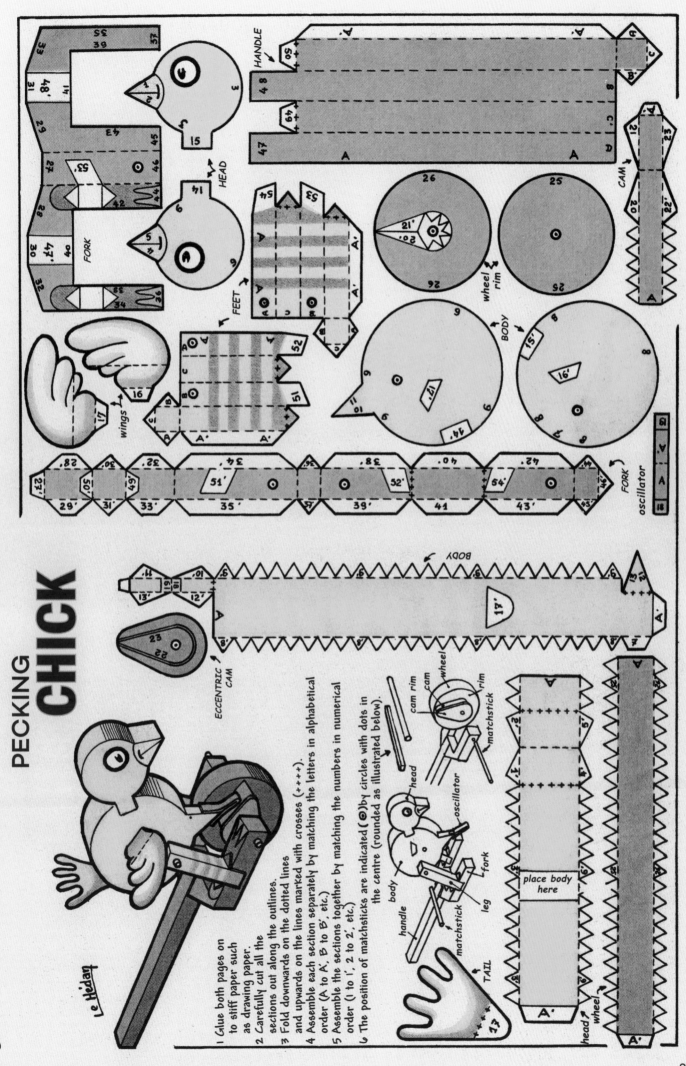

PECKING CHICK

Le Hédan

1 Glue both pages on to stiff paper such as drawing paper.

2 Carefully cut all the sections out along the outlines.

3 Fold downwards on the dotted lines and upwards on the lines marked with crosses (+ + + +).

4 Assemble each section separately by matching the letters in alphabetical order (A to A', B to B', etc.)

5 Assemble the sections together by matching the numbers in numerical order (1 to 1', 2 to 2', etc.)

6 The position of matchsticks are indicated (⊙) by circles with dots in the centre (rounded as illustrated below).

HOPPING HARE

Glue both pages on to fairly stiff paper such as drawing paper.

Cut all the sections out along the outlines.

Fold downwards on the dotted lines and upwards on the lines marked with crosses (+++).

Assemble each section separately by matching the letters in alphabetical order (A to A', B to B', etc.).

Assemble the sections together by matching the numbers in numerical order (1 to 1', 2 to 2', etc.).

Circles with dots in the centre indicate the position of axles (matchsticks).

CAM WHEEL

glue back to back

WASHER

SPACERS

WASHER

FRONT WHEEL

cam

FRONT WHEEL

glue back to back

HOOK

WHEEL TREADS

hook

WHEEL

WASHER

WASHER

matchstick axle

1 cam

STRUT

glued matchstick

spacers

2 cam

FRONT WHEEL

cam

STRUTS

BASE

99

STEAM Train

TOY to CUT OUT

Before cutting out, glue both pages on to thin card.

Fold the points downwards and use this disc to top off the funnel.

Roll into a funnel, fold the points inwards and glue to **A**

Make a cylinder, fold the points inwards and glue to **C**

glue this strip to the opposite edge to for a cylinder

put glue this part before positioning it on the base

put glue this part before positioning it on the base

A

B

top (to be glued)

make a cylinder and glue to **B**

fold

fold

fold

the boiler goes here

make 3 incisions to ensure the cyclinder sits securely on the base

J

K

E

D

F

L

M

glue

glue

fold

fold

fold

PLM

C

PLM

E

D

F

Glue tabs to **J** & **K** the vertical sides of the locomotive chassis.

Emergency wheel for the locomotive (in case of accidents when cutting out).

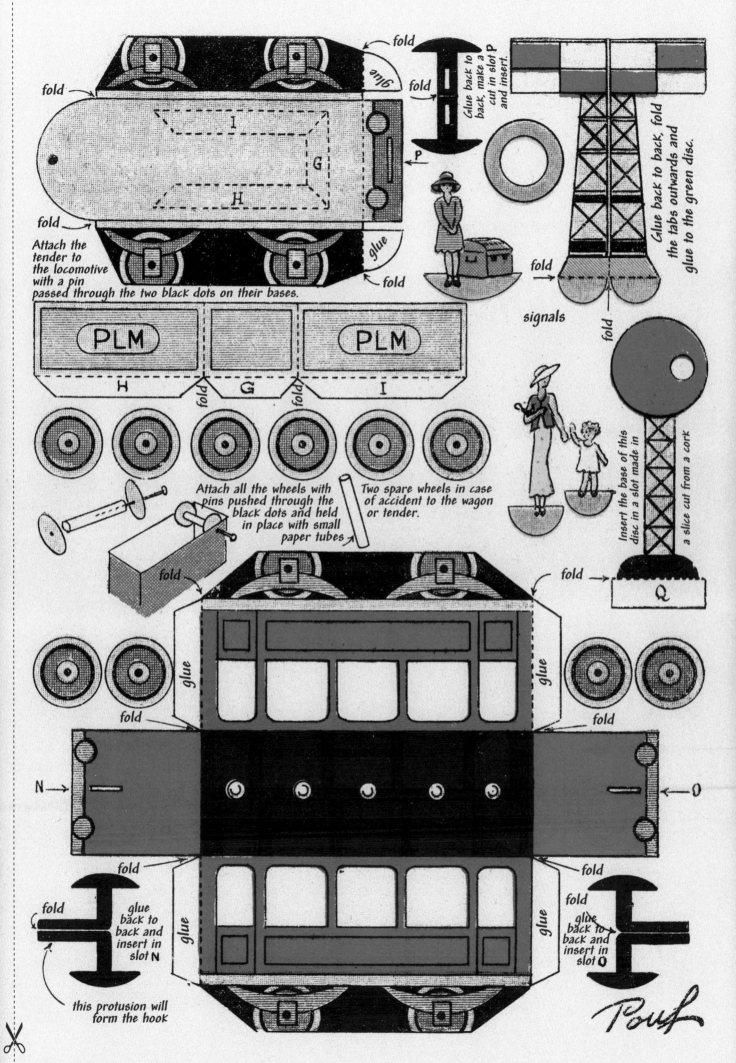

fold

fold

glue

fold

Glue back to back, make a cut in slot P and insert.

fold

P

Glue back to back, fold the tabs outwards and glue to the green disc.

fold

fold

signals

fold

Attach the tender to the locomotive with a pin passed through the two black dots on their bases.

PLM

PLM

H

fold

G

fold

I

Insert the base of this disc in a slot made in

a slice cut from a cork

Q

Attach all the wheels with pins pushed through the black dots and held in place with small paper tubes

Two spare wheels in case of accident to the wagon or tender.

fold

fold

glue

glue

fold

fold

N →

← O

fold

fold

fold

glue

glue

fold

fold

glue back to back and insert in slot N

glue back to back and insert in slot O

this protusion will form the hook

Pouf

103

LE MISTRAL

NO GLUING REQUIRED

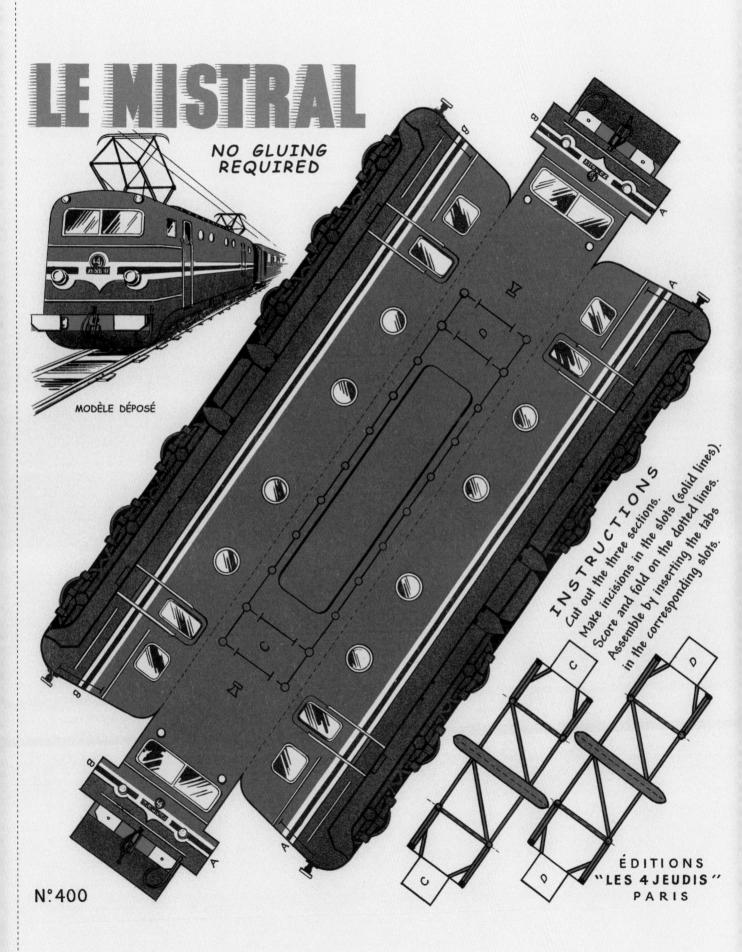

MODÈLE DÉPOSÉ

INSTRUCTIONS

Cut out the three sections.
Make incisions in the slots (solid lines).
Score and fold on the dotted lines.
Assemble by inserting the tabs
in the corresponding slots.

N° 400

ÉDITIONS
"LES 4 JEUDIS"
PARIS

AQUAPLANE
NO GLUING REQUIRED

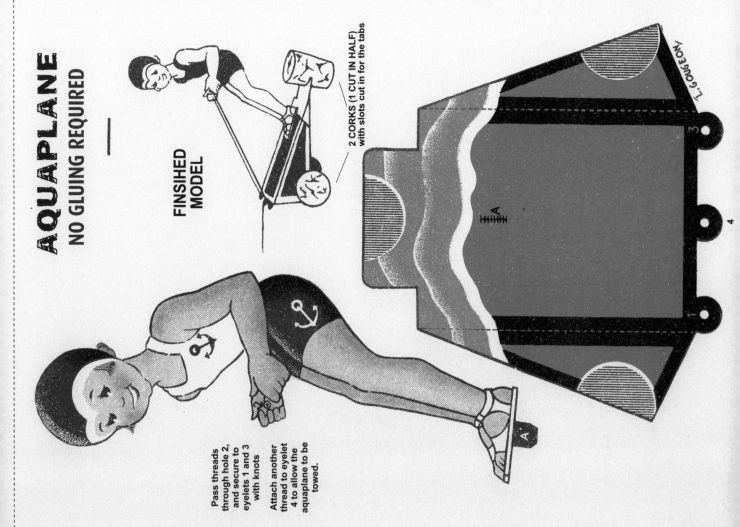

FINSIHED MODEL

2 CORKS (1 CUT IN HALF) with slots cut in for the tabs

Pass threads through hole 2, and secure to eyelets 1 and 3 with knots

Attach another thread to eyelet 4 to allow the aquaplane to be towed.

DINGHY
NO GLUING REQUIRED

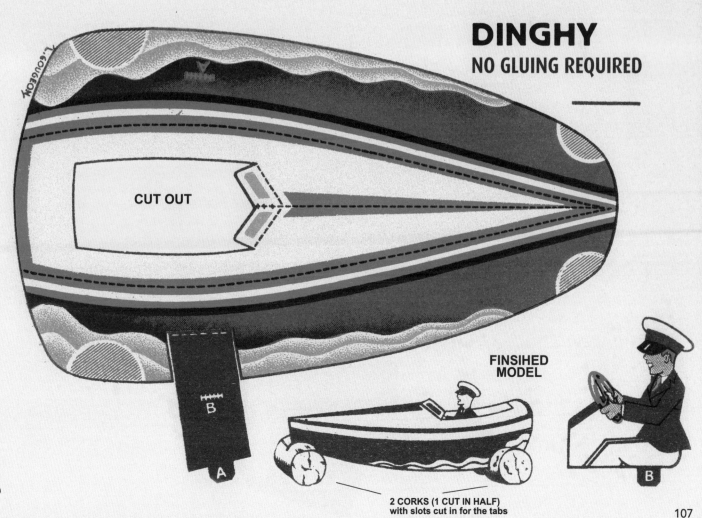

CUT OUT

FINSIHED MODEL

2 CORKS (1 CUT IN HALF) with slots cut in for the tabs

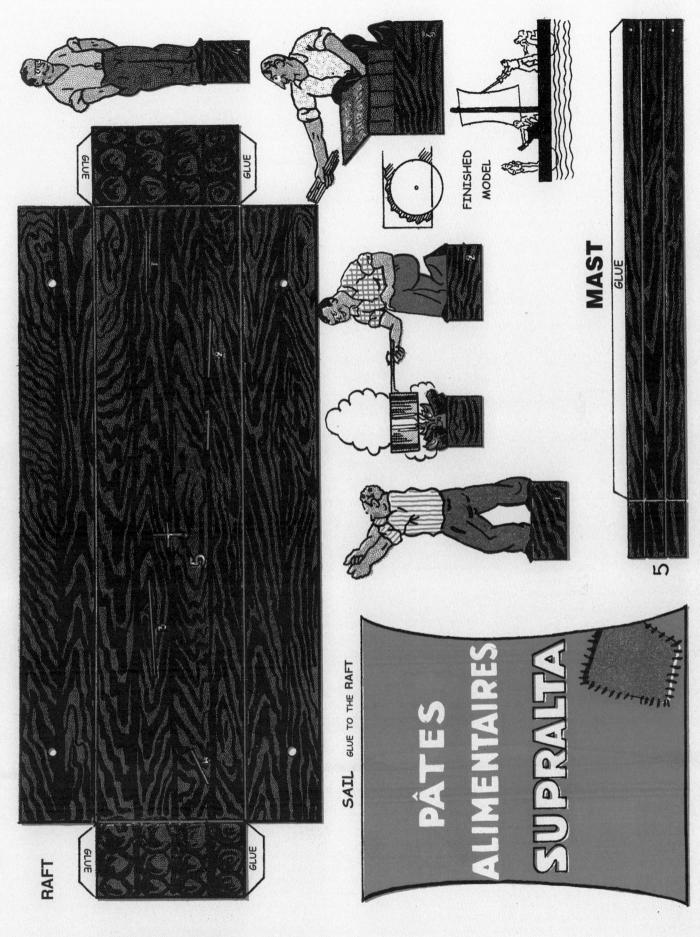

GLUE

GLUE

GLUE

GLUE

RAFT

GLUE

GLUE

SAIL GLUE TO THE RAFT

PÂTES
ALIMENTAIRES
SUPRALTA

FINISHED MODEL

MAST

GLUE

5

CUT OUT: **RAFT**

1 Carefully cut out all the pieces. Have ready two corks and four pins.

2 Assemble the cut-out pieces according to the illustration. Glue the figures and other pieces in the positions marked.

3 Position the corks as shown and attach them to the underside of the raft with pins, one at each end.

4 Pass a thread between the top of the mast and the hands of figure 1.

With this rigging the raft will float.

24-Cannon C'hébec Sailing Ship
1750

scale : 1:600

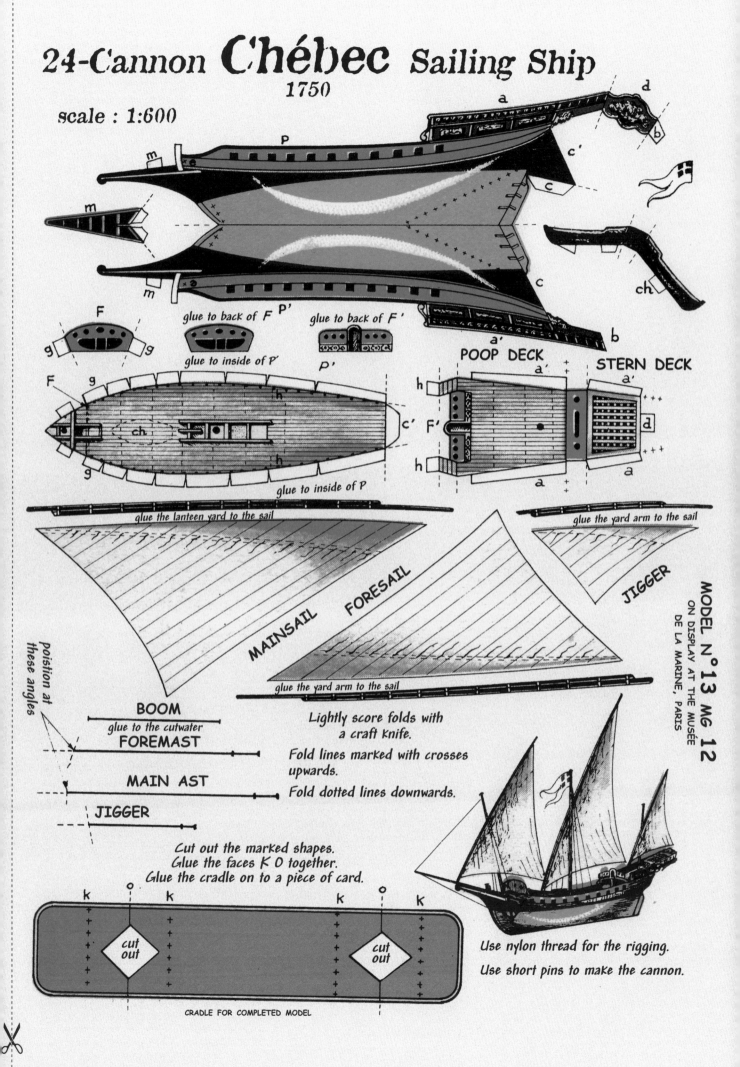

P

m

m

m

a

d

b

c'

c

c

ch

F

g g

glue to back of F **P'**

glue to back of F'

glue to inside of P'

P'

glue to back of F'

glue to inside of P'

a'

b

POOP DECK

STERN DECK

F

g

F

g

ch

h

h

glue to inside of P

h

F'

h

a'

a'

d

a

a

glue the lanteen yard to the sail

glue the yard arm to the sail

MAINSAIL

FORESAIL

JIGGER

glue the yard arm to the sail

position at
these angles

BOOM

glue to the cutwater

FOREMAST

MAIN AST

JIGGER

Lightly score folds with
a craft knife.

Fold lines marked with crosses
upwards.

Fold dotted lines downwards.

MODEL N°13 MG 12

ON DISPLAY AT THE MUSÉE
DE LA MARINE, PARIS

Cut out the marked shapes.
Glue the faces K O together.
Glue the cradle on to a piece of card.

k   o   k   k   o   k

cut
out

cut
out

CRADLE FOR COMPLETED MODEL

Use nylon thread for the rigging.

Use short pins to make the cannon.

111

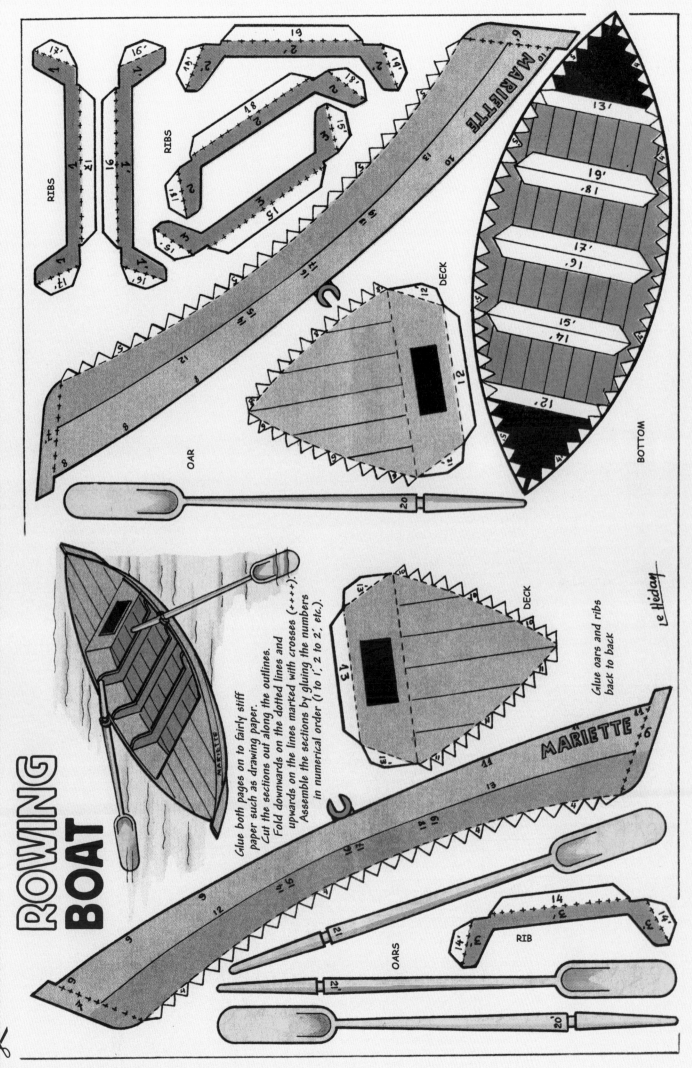

ROWING BOAT

RIBS

RIBS

MARIETTE

DECK

OAR

BOTTOM

Glue both pages on to fairly stiff
paper such as drawing paper.
Cut the sections out along the outlines.
Fold downwards on the dotted lines and
upwards on the lines marked with crosses (++++).
Assemble the sections by gluing the numbers
in numerical order (1 to 1', 2 to 2', etc.).

Glue oars and ribs
back to back

MARIETTE

DECK

OARS

RIB

le Héday

STEAM LAUNCH

Cut the sections out along the outlines, cutting round the tabs.
Fold on the dotted lines.
Assemble by matching the letters.

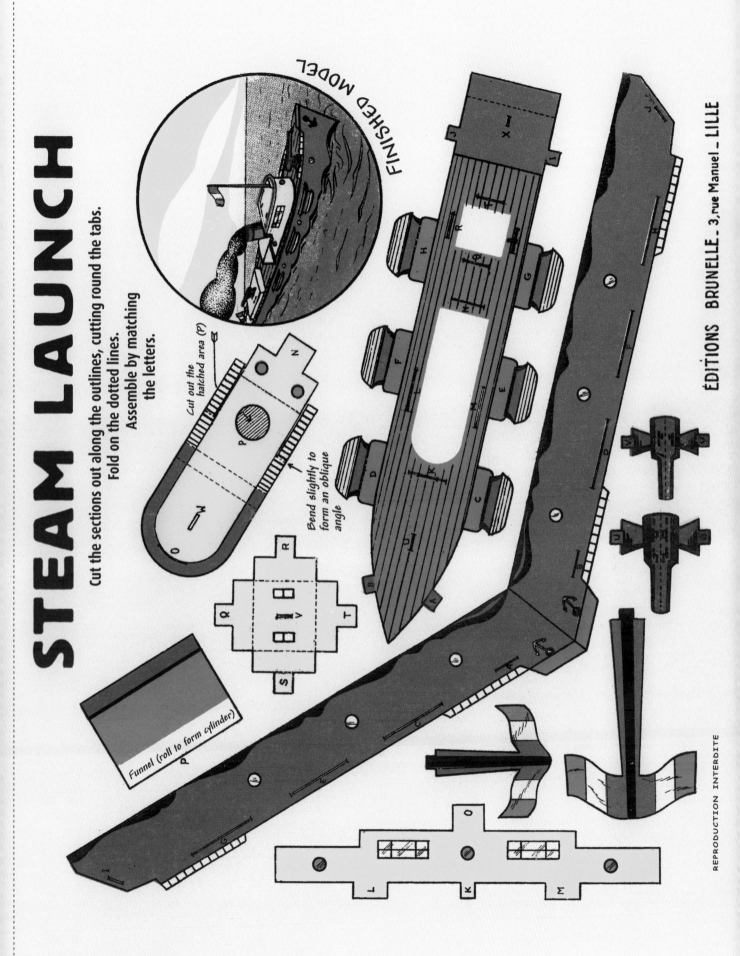

FINISHED MODEL

Cut out the hatched area (P)

Bend slightly to form an oblique angle

Funnel (roll to form cylinder)

✂ No gluing required

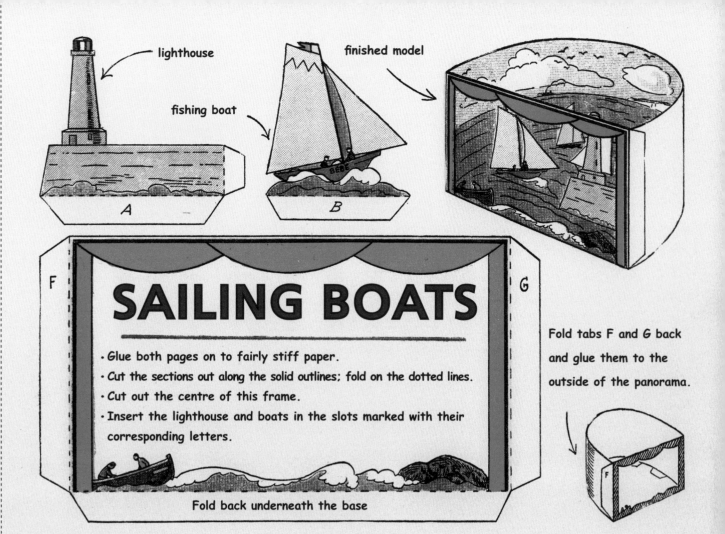

lighthouse

finished model

fishing boat

F

G

SAILING BOATS

- Glue both pages on to fairly stiff paper.
- Cut the sections out along the solid outlines; fold on the dotted lines.
- Cut out the centre of this frame.
- Insert the lighthouse and boats in the slots marked with their corresponding letters.

Fold back underneath the base

Fold tabs F and G back and glue them to the outside of the panorama.

F

J K L L M R

All at Sea

Construction

tab O · **tab C** · **tab F** · **tab E**

tab A

tab D

tab B.

1. With a craft knife, cut the slots indicated in the sea. Fold the sea forwards. Fold supports A and B back on either side of the backdrop.
2. Before cutting the other sections out, score the folds of the tabs with the point of a craft knife. Bend the tabs backwards at right angles and insert them into the slots with the corresponding letters.

· SOUVENIR DE LA BELLE JARDINIÈRE ·

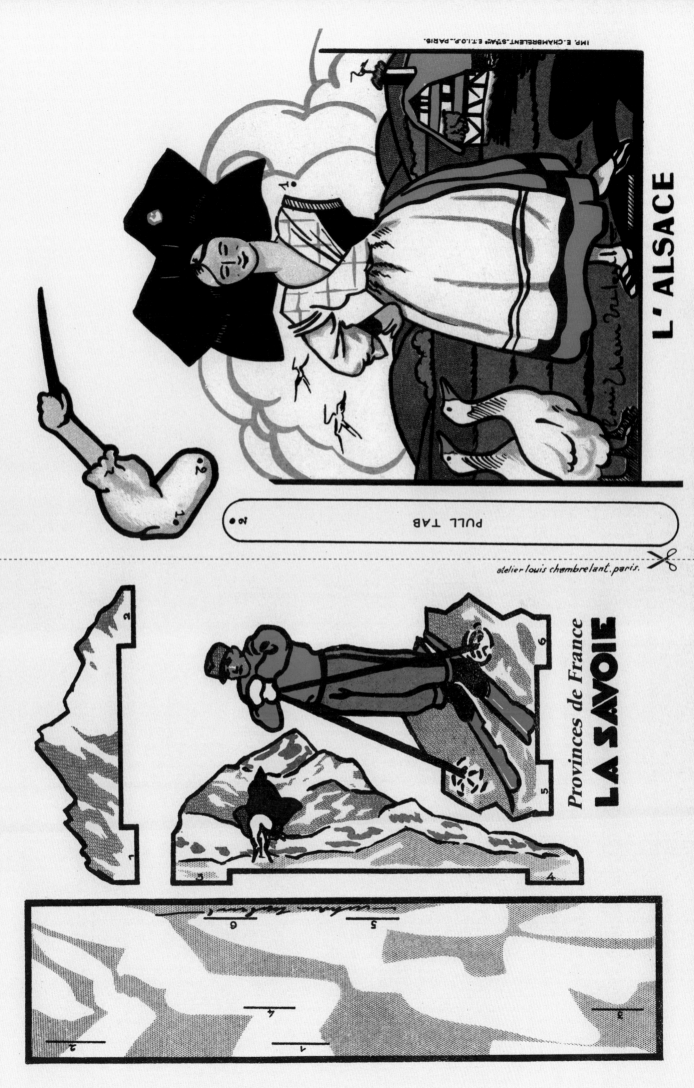

L' ALSACE

PULL TAB

IMP. E. CHAMBRELENT-STAP. ET L.O.P., PARIS.

atelier louis chambrelant, paris.

Provinces de France
LA SAVOIE

121

Glue on to stiff paper and cut out the figures and their bases. Make the figures stand on their bases by folding back the tabs.

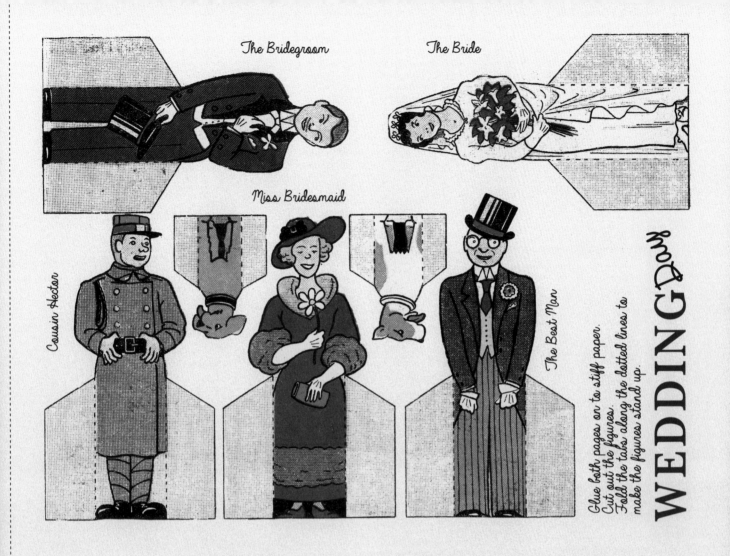

The Bridegroom

The Bride

Miss Bridesmaid

Cousin Hector

The Best Man

WEDDING Day

Glue both pages on to stiff paper.
Cut out the figures.
Fold the tabs along the dotted lines to
make the figures stand up.

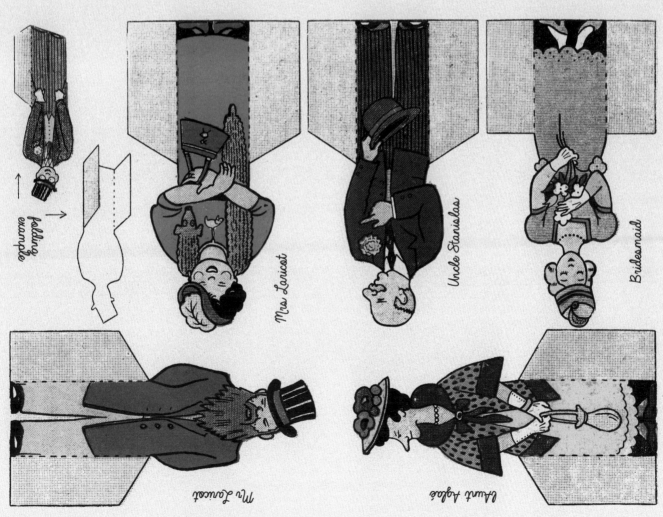

folding example

Mrs Laricot

Uncle Stanislas

Bridesmaid

Mr Laricot

Aunt Aglaé

125

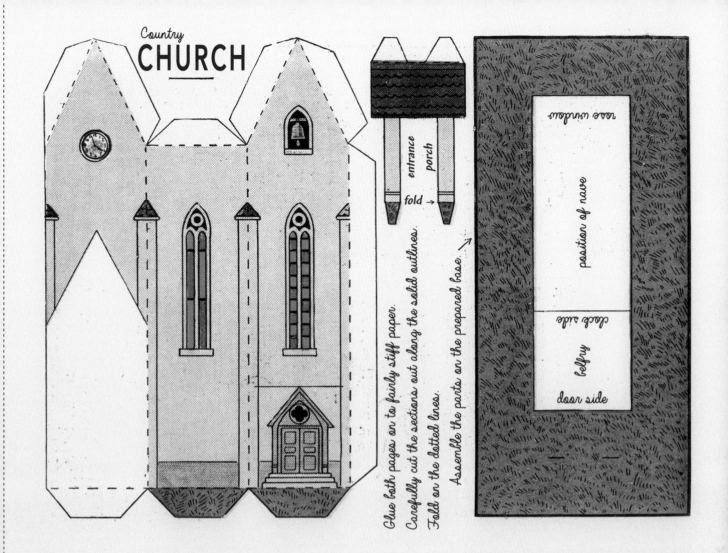

entrance
porch

fold →

Glue both pages on to fairly stiff paper.
Carefully cut the sections out along the solid outlines.
Fold on the dotted lines.
Assemble the parts on the prepared base.

rose window

position of nave

door side

belfry

door side

belfry roof →

nave roof →

finished model ←

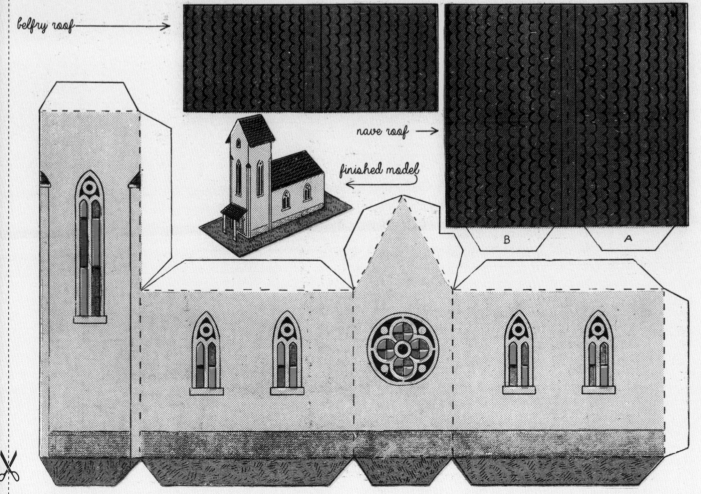

B

A

the **WOLF** &
the *Lamb*

CRÉÉ ET ÉDITÉ PAR "LES 4 JEUDIS" 12, RUE DU HAVRE, PARIS MODÈLE DÉPOSÉ

Cut out the sections, then fold and assemble them as shown in the illustration, matching the numbers.

N° 75

MONTAGE *Eclair*

TOM THUMB

PAUL GIRAUD

Cut out the sections and assemble them by inserting the slots of bushes A, B and C into the slots in the backdrop. Cut the background (P) from one side of a cardboard box, glue the copse to it and add clouds or other features. Make folds at E, F, G and H, and arrange the rest of the model on the adjoining side (at right angles) and scatter with fine gravel.

CUT OUT

THE WOLF &
THE CRANE

PAUL GIRAUD

DR CRANE FOR SORE THROATS

Cut out the sections and assemble them by inserting the slots of bushes A, B and C into slots A, B and C. Make folds at DE and FG to make the sections stand up. Make the vertical background (P) by cutting out one side of a cardboard box, glue section R to it and draw in some clouds. Use the adjoining side of the box (at right angles) to make the ground and scatter with grass and fine gravel.

fold and glue
back to back

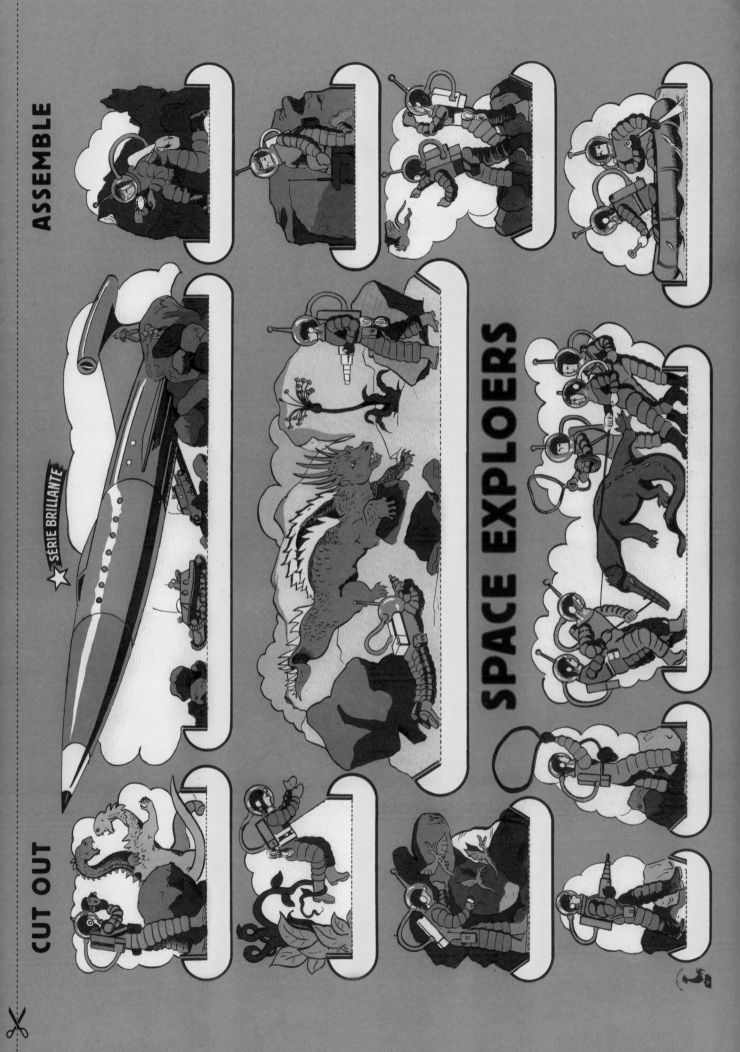

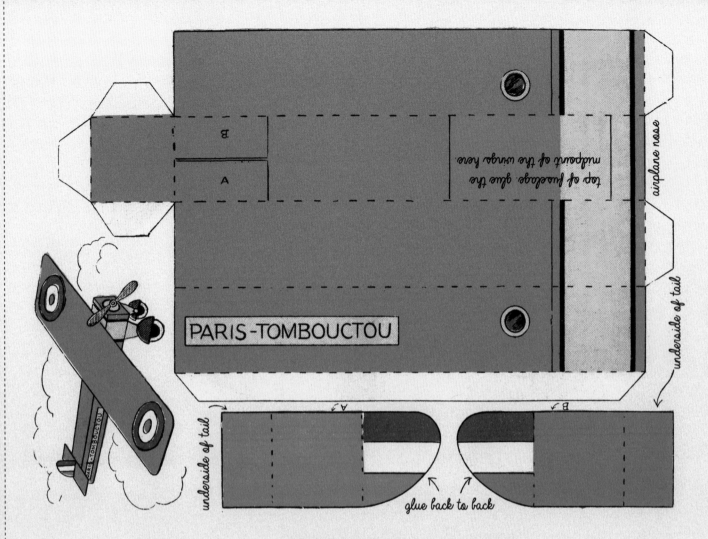

PARIS-TOMBOUCTOU

airplane nose

top of fuselage glue the
midpoint of the wings here

underside of tail

underside of tail

glue back to back

TOY PLANE

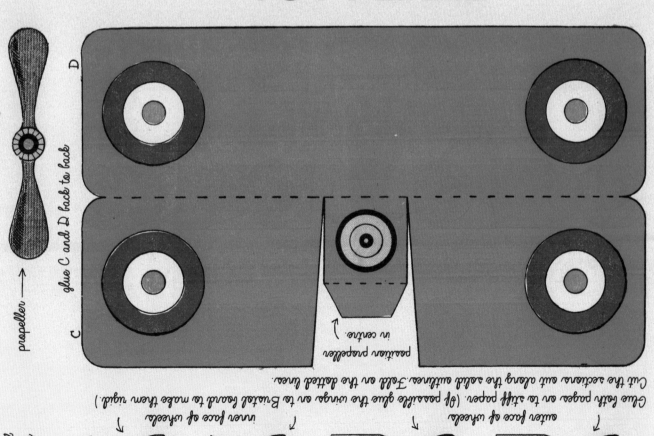

propeller →

glue C and D back to back

position propeller
in centre

Cut the sections out along the solid outlines. Fold on the dotted lines.
Glue both pages on to stiff paper. (If possible glue the wings on to Bristol board to make them rigid.)

outer face of wheels   inner face of wheels

Hang the model
from the ceiling
with a thread.

Modern Transport

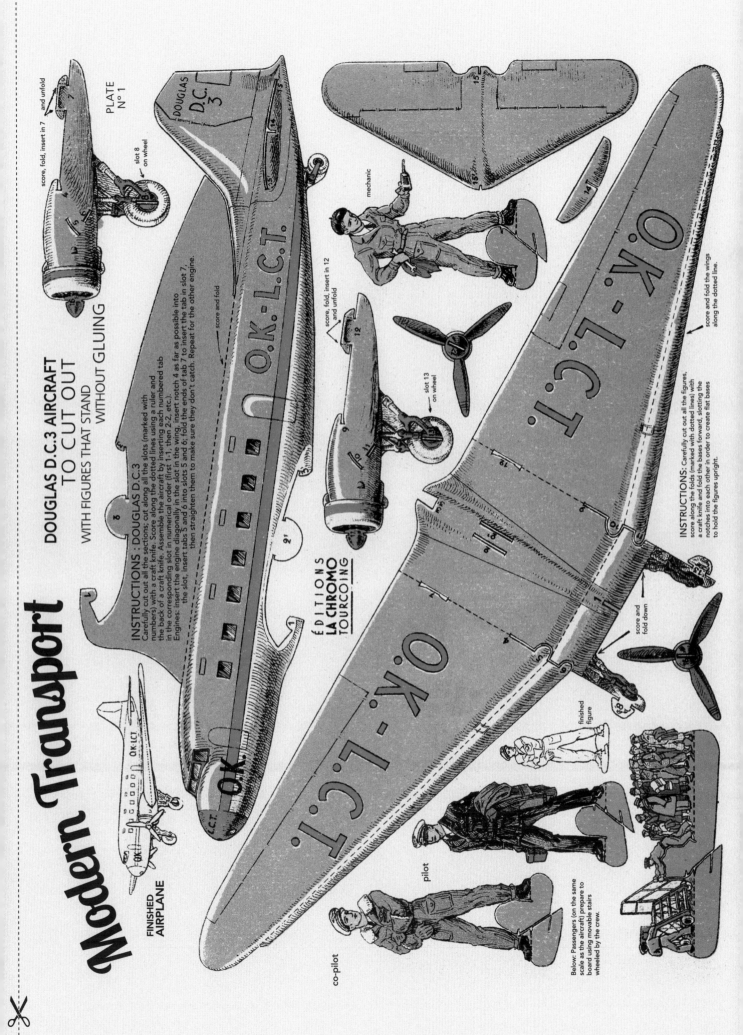

DOUGLAS D.C.3 AIRCRAFT
TO CUT OUT
WITH FIGURES THAT STAND
WITHOUT GLUING

FINISHED AIRPLANE

INSTRUCTIONS : DOUGLAS D.C.3

Carefully cut out all the sections; cut along all the slots (marked with numbers) with a craft knife. Score along the dotted lines using a ruler and the back of a craft knife. Assemble the aircraft by inserting each numbered tab in the corresponding slot in numerical order (first 1-1, then 2-2, etc.).
Engines: insert the engine diagonally in the slot in the wing, insert notch 4 as far as possible into the slot, insert tabs 5 and 6 into slots 5 and 6; fold the ends of tab 7 to insert the tab in slot 7. then straighten them to make sure they don't catch. Repeat for the other engine.

score and fold

ÉDITIONS
LA CHROMO
TOURCOING

PLATE
N° 1

score, fold, insert in 7 and unfold

slot 8 on wheel

DOUGLAS
D.C.
3

O·K·-L·C·T.

O.K.

L.C.T.

O·K·-L·C·T.

mechanic

score, fold, insert in 12 and unfold

slot 13 on wheel

15

15

14

O·K·-L·C·T.

O·K·-L·C·T.

score and fold the wings along the dotted line.

INSTRUCTIONS: Carefully cut out all the figures, score along the folds (marked with dotted lines) with a craft knife and fold the bases forward, slotting the notches into each other in order to create flat bases to hold the figures upright.

score and fold down

finished figure

pilot

co-pilot

Below: Passengers (on the same scale as the aircraft) prepare to board using movable stairs wheeled by the crew.

139

BUILD A
LIGHT AIRCRAFT

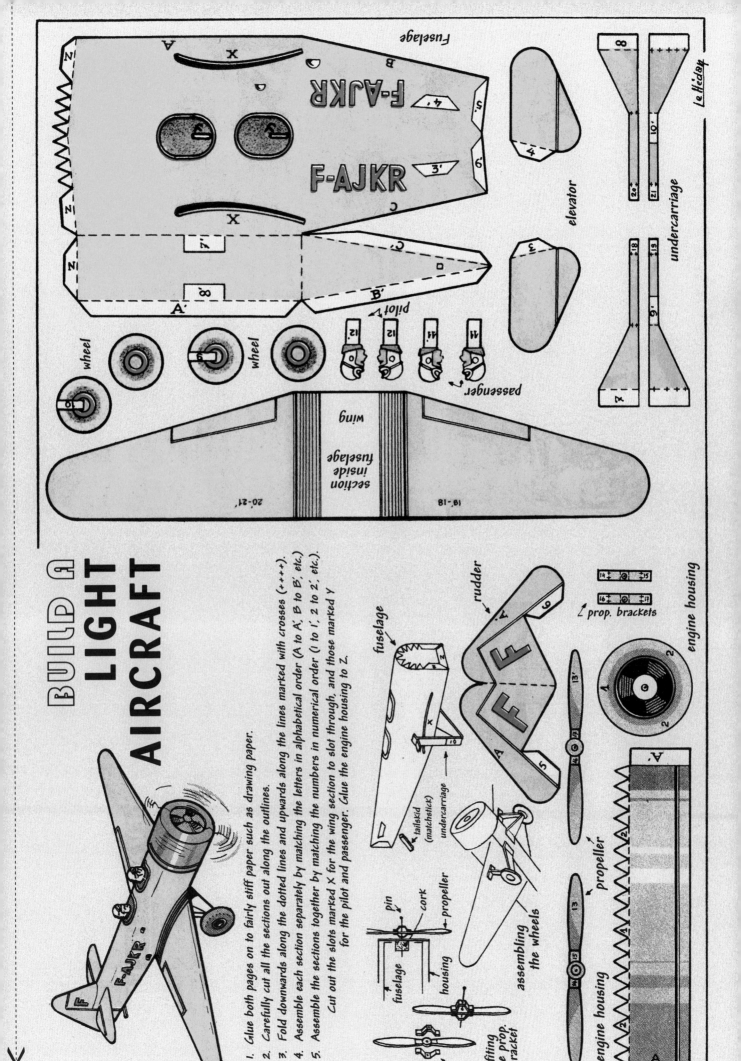

1. Glue both pages on to fairly stiff paper such as drawing paper.
2. Carefully cut all the sections out along the outlines.
3. Fold downwards along the dotted lines and upwards along the lines marked with crosses (+++).
4. Assemble each section separately by matching the letters in alphabetical order (A to A´, B to B´, etc.).
5. Assemble the sections together by matching the numbers in numerical order (1 to 1´, 2 to 2´, etc.).

Cut out the slots marked X for the wing section to slot through, and those marked Y for the pilot and passenger. Glue the engine housing to Z.

F-AJKR

F-AJKR

fuselage

fuselage

elevator

undercarriage

wheel

wheel

pilot

passenger

wing

section inside fuselage

rudder

prop. brackets

engine housing

engine housing

fuselage

tailskid (matchstick)

undercarriage

assembling the wheels

pin

cork

propeller

fuselage

housing

fitting the prop. bracket

prop. bracket

propeller

propeller

AERODROME

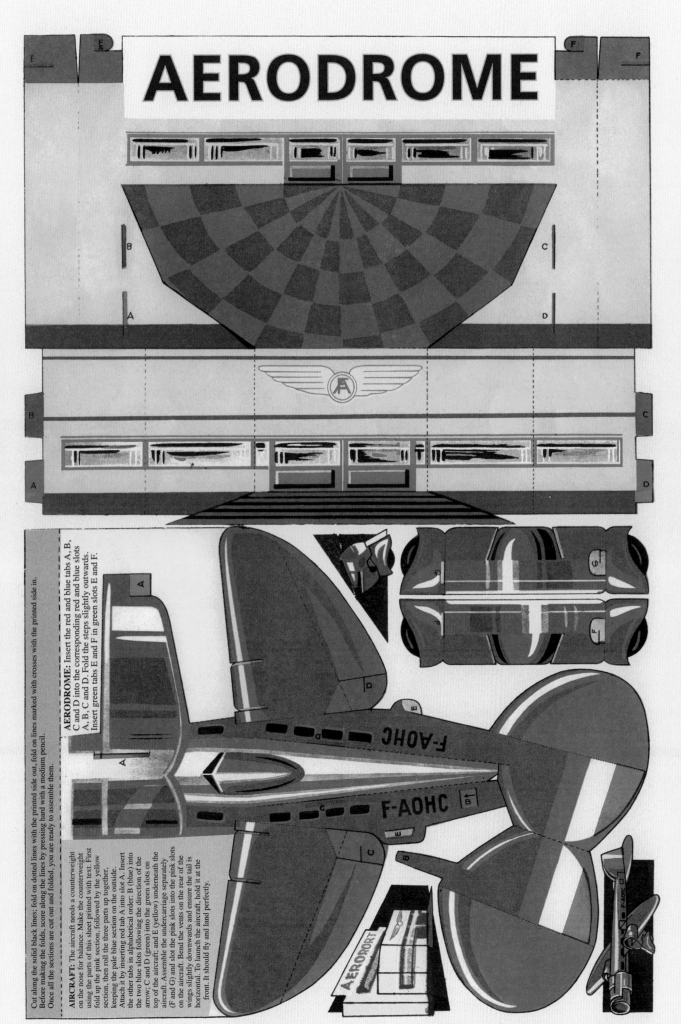

Cut along the solid black lines; fold on dotted lines with the printed side in, fold on lines marked with crosses with the printed side in. Before making the folds, score along the lines by pressing hard with a medium pencil. Once all the sections are cut out and folded, you are ready to assemble them.

AIRCRAFT: The aircraft needs a counterweight on the nose for balance. Make the counterweight using the parts of this sheet printed with text. First fold up the pink section, followed by the yellow section, then roll the three parts up together, keeping the pale blue section on the outside.

Attach it by inserting red tab A into slot A. Insert the other tabs in alphabetical order: B (blue) into the two blue slots following the direction of the arrow; C and D (green) into the green slots on top of the aircraft; and E (yellow) underneath the aircraft. Assemble the undercarriage separately (F and G) and slot the pink slots into the pink slots on the aircraft. Bend the vents on the rear of the wings slightly downwards and ensure the tail is horizontal. To launch the aircraft, hold it at the front. It should fly and land perfectly.

AERODROME: Insert the red and blue tabs A, B, C and D into the corresponding red and blue slots A, B, C and D. Fold the steps slightly outwards. Insert green tabs E and F in green slots E and F.

WOOD-MILNE PAPER PLANE

FLIES VERY WELL BUT WILL FLY EVEN BETTER IF WOOD-MILNE SOLES AND HEELS ARE USED!

ASSEMBLY

Cut out the four sections along the black lines.
Fold the fuselage along the lines 5-511 and A-B. Insert wing notches 1-111 and 2-211 into the corresponding fuselage notches. Follow the same procedure for the tail fin, notches 3 and 311. Insert rudder section 4 into fuselage slot 4. Attach several pins or a paperclip to the nose of the plane to balance its flight. Adjust the front and rear ailerons to achieve a wide range of manoeuvres.

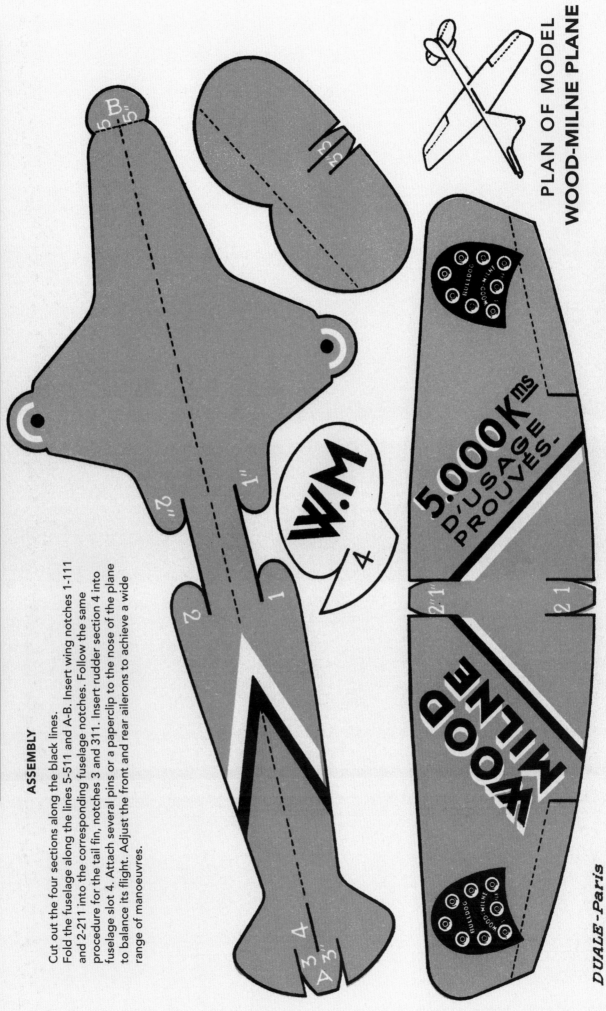

PLAN OF MODEL
WOOD-MILNE PLANE

DUALE - Paris

145

ALGÉSAL *souplesse des articulations*

PUNCH. (Puppet.)

ALGÉSAL

souplesse des articulations

ALGÉSAL

souplesse des articulations

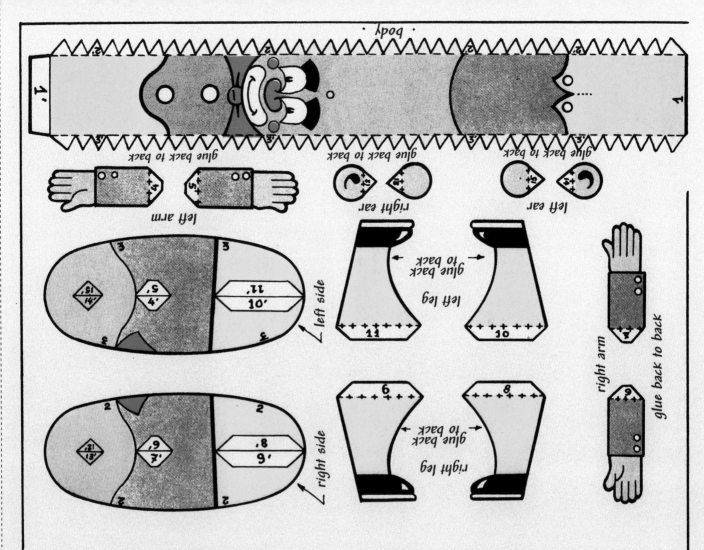

MAKE YOUR OWN WOBBLY MAN

1. Glue the opposite page on to fairly stiff paper such as drawing paper.
2. Carefully cut all the sections out along the outlines.
3. Attach the forelock (made from strands of wool).
4. Fold upwards along the dotted lines
5. Fold downwards along the lines marked with crosses (+++).
6. Assemble the sections by matching the numbers in numerical order (1 to 1′, 2 to 2′, etc.).
   Remember to place a large, heavy marble inside the body.

strands of wool

glue

marble

left side — body

Place the marble inside the body before finally gluing it.

Put the wobbly man at the top of a slight slope and watch him perform somersaults.

PIGGY BANK

THAT SAYS THANK YOU

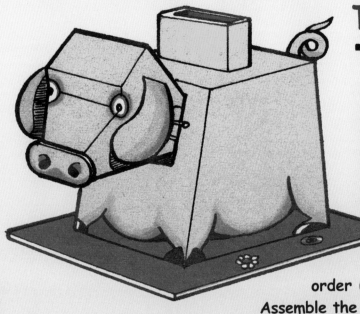

Glue both pages on to fairly stiff
paper such as drawing paper.
Glue the base on to cardboard.
Cut the sections out along the outlines.
Fold the dotted lines downwards.
Fold the lines marked with crosses
(++++) upwards.
Assemble each section separately
by matching the letters in alphabetical
order (A to A1, B to B1, etc.).
Assemble the sections together by matching the
numbers in numerical order (1 to 11, 2 to 21, etc.).
Circles with dots in the centre indicate where pins go.
Drop coins into the piggy bank through the coin slot.

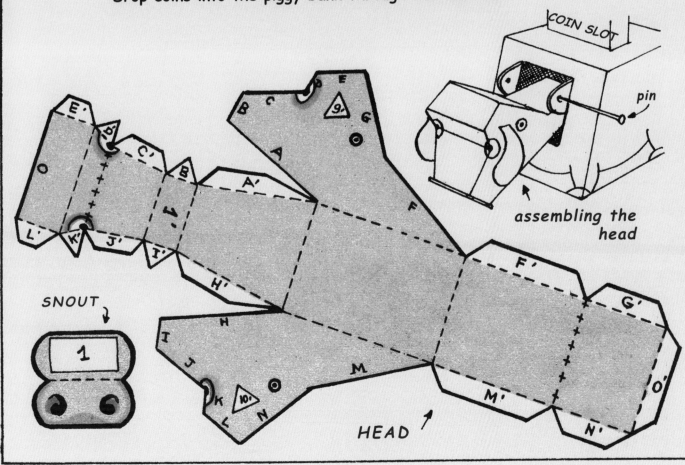

assembling the
head

SNOUT

HEAD

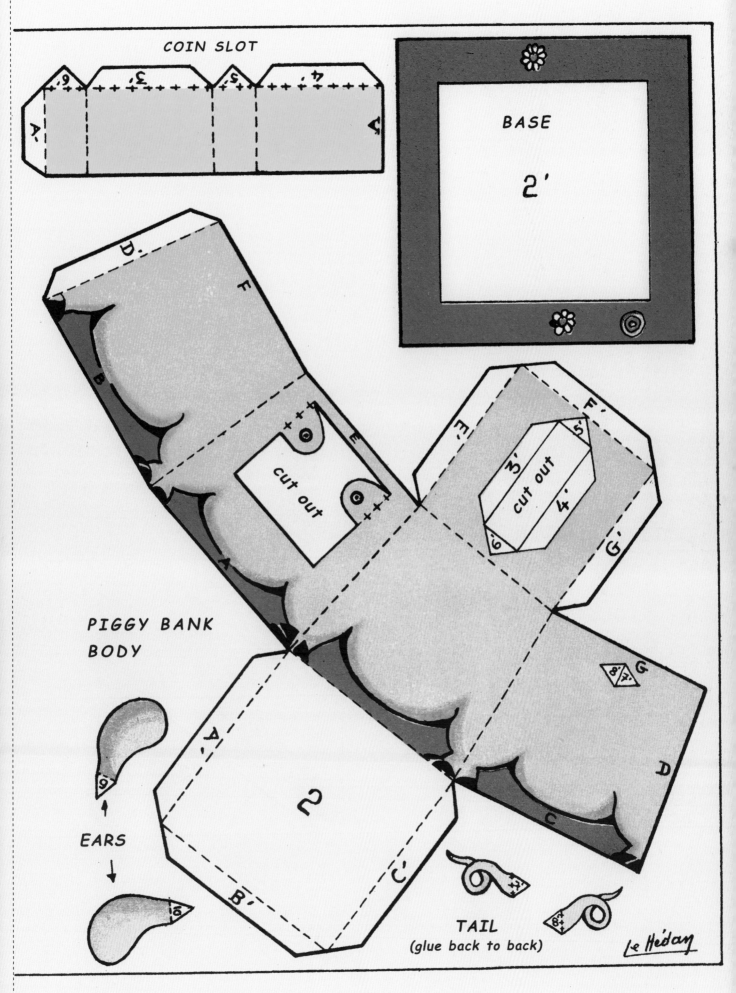

COIN SLOT

BASE

2'

PIGGY BANK
BODY

cut out

cut out

EARS

TAIL
(glue back to back)

Le Hédan

All the images are from the Éditions du Chêne private collection.

Published by **Scriptum Editions**, 2015
An imprint of **Co & Bear Productions (UK) Ltd**
63 Edith Grove, London, SW10 0LB
www.scriptumeditions.co.uk

Publishers: Beatrice Vincenzini & Francesco Venturi
Translation into English: Barbara Mellor
Managing Editor: Flavie Gaidon
Editor and Research: Franck Friès
Art Director: Sabine Houplain,
assisted by Claire Mieyeville
Cover Design: Atelier Saje
Layout and Repro: Les PAOistes

First published, in French, by **Editions du Chêne – Hachette Livre**, 2014

Original title: **PAPER TOYS**: Vintage
©**Editions du Chêne – Hachette Livre**, 2014, for the original work.
Translation ©**Co&Bear Productions (UK) Ltd**

Distributed by **Thames & Hudson**

10 9 8 7 6 5 4 3 2 1

ISBN: 978-1-902686-83-7

Printed in Malaysia